# Transparency in ESG and the Circular Economy

D1294282

# Transparency in ESG and the Circular Economy

*Capturing Opportunities Through Data*

Cristina Dolan and Diana Barrero Zalles

BUSINESS EXPERT PRESS
*Leader in applied, concise business books*

*As the world continues to transform at an accelerated pace, I dedicate this book to my sons, Teddy and Cristiaan Fitzsimons, who will be inheriting a very different world. Thank you both for always inspiring me, and as the Dr. Seuss quote from the Lorax states, "It's not about what it is, it's about what it can become." Never stop believing in your ability to make dreams come true!*

—Cristina

*To all those who helped make this book possible and who believed in me along the journey. Your encouragement and support mean the world!*

—Diana

# Description

This book is not a "how to" manual to propose yet another ESG framework. It focuses on the "what" and the "why" of the matter, in order to remove ambiguities, and presents the role of emerging technologies to manage ESG data and provide better understanding through transparency and accountability. It takes the perspective of a company seeking to attract ESG investments and become compliant with ESG regulatory requirements. It proposes the following main points:

1. **Understanding ESG:** ESG is a very broad topic that companies can implement adequately by integrating it into their existing strategic business operations. This requires buy-in at the governance level, integration across the corporate culture, and a long-term view.
2. **Disregarding ESG Means Risk:** Companies are experiencing pressure from several fronts to improve their ESG practices and reduce material financial risks. Today cybersecurity is particularly relevant.
3. **Inconsistent Metrics & Lack of Clarity:** Different approaches can rate the same company very differently. This can allow for inaccurate reporting such as greenwashing. It is also difficult to form a holistic view of the full ESG impact of an activity. For instance, an operation or product may be climate friendly, but the supply chain may create emissions, and management may be oblivious to labor standards.
4. **Technology to Organize Data:** In order to make changes, it is crucial to understand and measure the underlying problems. IoT can capture various data points. Distributed ledgers can record data and connect the various facets of ESG impact, capturing journeys of data to provide a holistic view. AI and Machine Learning can draw insights for improvement and iteration. While a convergence of frameworks can ensure breadth of data across major issues, we also need a level of granularity to allow investment approaches focused on specific topics.

5. **What Companies can do to be ESG-Investable & ESG-Compliant:** Regulations are ramping up ESG requirements, and public companies are rolling up the data and numbers. Large companies are requiring small suppliers and young tech partners to commit to their 'corporate sustainability' practices. Looking ahead, trends toward ESG practices can support a new generation of "sustainability native" startups.

# Keywords

ESG; environmental social governance; sustainability; UN sustainable development goals; cybersecurity; data security; circular economy; ESG data; climate tech; sustainable funds; sustainable investment; ESG standards; greenwashing

# Contents

# Testimonials

*"ESG may not be a new concept but it's necessary for today's economy. This book does a tremendous job laying out the history of ESG, why it's vitally important for investors and citizens today, and most importantly, how to measure it. This book fills in the required gap of outlining how to effectively and fairly measure ESG, doing so from a data driven and transparency perspective that is not only unique but unparalleled in its depth, intelligence and awareness of the impact that ESG can have in our world going forward."*—**Jack Tatar, co-author of** *Cryptoassets: The Innovative Investor's Guide to Bitcoin and Beyond*

*"A very important and timely book that explains the evolution of the ESG data landscape and its relevance for decision making. An amazingly comprehensive analysis of how sustainable investing is evolving, this book explains with great clarity what matters for professionals and decision makers. As sustainability is reshaping the world of finance, this book offers a timely and highly relevant overview of trends and insights professionals and decision makers need to know."*—**Georg Kell, Chairman of the Board at Arabesque, Founding Director of the United Nations Global Compact**

*"ESG attempts to redefine and expand the definition of a corporate stakeholder. Releasing an expanded view on opportunities, challenges, rewards and consequences. This book provides a much needed holistic view of how the disparate attempts to codify a cohesive and mainstream framework are gaining momentum but still in the early stages."*—**Rich Radice, CFO, Moven Bank**

*"Humanity sits at the convergence of two massively transformative trends that urgently demand a cohesive, collective response. The first is the rapid expansion of interconnected digital technologies and in the data they generate. The second is the rapid progression of climate change and the threat it poses to societies. To say, the first should be marshaled to address the second goes without*

*saying. The challenge is to put all that digital data and computing capacity into a common ESG framework that produces consistent, coordinated actions by companies and investors, even as they face competing interests and operate in independent jurisdictions. In this vital, timely book, the authors produce a clear-headed manual for achieving that, one that cuts through all the acronyms and confusing taxonomy to point to a path forward."*—**Michael Casey, Chief Content Officer, CoinDesk, co-author of *The Truth Machine: the Blockchain and the Future of Everything***

*"Trust is critical in the transforming world economy, shaped by new business models built on next generation technologies that enable unprecedented connectivity across a wide range of stakeholders across the globe. Yet how do we uphold good business practices consistently, particularly when it comes to data privacy and security, when often, standards are fragmented across sectors and geographies? Stakeholders remain on different "islands," subject to vastly different metrics and approaches to data. This critical book brings light to the role of emerging technologies to consolidate data and maximize the benefits of understanding such data better, which is fundamental for implementing sustainable operations, spanning from all aspects of governance, environmental, and social practices, for the new class of businesses that will shape the future."*—**Sandra Ro, CEO, Global Blockchain Business Council**

*"This book is a must read for professional investors integrating ESG and sustainability factors to improve long-term investment outcomes. Dolan and Barrero Zalles brilliantly dissect sustainable data, from frameworks to standards, critical for analysis and decisions."*—**Carole K. Crawford, CFA, Managing Partner, fincap360**

*"I highly recommend this book for anyone who is confused about all the conflicting information on ESG. Measurement of ESG will be a necessary skill set for investors in this decade. It will be very helpful to be ahead of the curve by reading this book."*—**Peter C. Fusaro, Senior Partner, ESG, Oxford Global Accelerated Ventures**

*"ESG is investment destiny; there's no escaping its growing influence and importance. Understanding the politics, economics and dynamics of 'data' is essential to grasping the ESG future. This remarkably incisive book is your manual for boosting 'Return on ESG.'"*—**Michael Schrage, Research Fellow with MIT Sloan School's Initiative on the Digital Economy**

*"Dolan and Barrero Zalles deliver a valuable resource for developing a strategic approach to ESG—Sustainability. They show the evolutionary path and timeline to today's high visibility, help navigate through a maze of acronyms and point the way to future direction."*—**Art Tauder, Former Vice-Chairman, The McCann WorldGroup**

*"Managing sustainability and ESG risk requires understanding of what it is and the components that contribute to the risk, like cyber security, which poses one of the greatest threats to organizations and governments. Dolan and Barrero Zalles have done an outstanding job of providing clarity around this complex and ambiguous topic as regulations for reporting increase. Managing requires understanding, and the book is a great place for executives, board members and students to start."*—**Carlos Moreira, Founder and CEO WISeKey International Holding**

*"Paraphrasing Einstein, 'We cannot solve our problems with the same thinking we used when we created them.' The current challenges of mass extinction, loss of biodiversity, oceans choking on plastic and waste, climate change, growing inequalities, among many other global problems, demand a different thinking that the linear extractive capitalist of the 1st, 2nd and 3rd industrial revolutions that originated them. ESG Compliance provides us this necessary new thinking, presenting 'Why to do it' in order to calibrate our inner compass. AI algorithms, working on mountains of Big Data, generated by billions of networked sensors and interconnected IoT devices adding meaningful information to the infinite blockchains, will be the smart exponential toolkit to make change happen toward a new circular, accountable and responsible data driven capitalism of this dawning new era. This book offers the reader a good starting point."*—**Ignacio Villoch, Open Innovation Senior Ecosystem Builder, BBVA**

*"The focus on ESG is non-negotiable in the valuation of companies and as determinant of their long term viability and vitality. It integrates stewardship of people and environment in the overall assessment of their risk and performance. This book illustrates the importance of ESG as a strategic priority, the challenges in implementing this on a holistic level, and the promise of emerging technologies to provide for transparency and accountability."*
—**Carolyn Woo, Board Member at Arabesque**

*"Dolan and Barrero Zalles provide a fascinating and timely overview of the rise of ESG importance, the rise of the CSO role in understanding and managing the data and avoiding Greenwashing. A clear and comprehensive overview of the history of ESG and the evolving standards. A first publication that provides a riveting account of the past, current and future challenges faced by firms and their supply chain, as they navigate issues from cyber security, better resource management and conforming to current and evolving ESG standards."*—**Aymen Andrew Samawi, former Managing Director at ICAP and current CEO of Geneva-based asset management**

*"If you want to be in business today and in the future it is critical to understand ESG, what it means, how it is implemented, and how it is tracked. Dolan and Barrero Zalles do a great job in outlining the components included in ESG programs today and the challenges that we face to get clear and consistent ways to measure this space. A valuable primer for anyone trying to get up to speed and ahead of ESG trends."*—**Bant Breen, Founder and Chairman, Qnary**

*"For a long time, measuring ESG impact has been nebulous, and has led to the false conclusion that funds chasing impact would be weaker on returns. That myth is finally debunked with data. So all of the allocators that equate investing in diversity/sustainability as charity work should read this excellent book."*—**Nisa Amoils, Managing Partner at A100x**

*"Outstanding analysis on sustainability and ESG metrics and evolution, Dolan and Barrero Zalles effectively show how companies' governance and ethics deeply impact the community, environment and ecosystem they are*

*part of and why understanding their data is critical to fight global threats like cyber security and climate change. A must for companies, investors and customers alike."*—**Carlos Jiménez, President of Secuware**

*"The most comprehensive and detailed analysis of the current state of ESG. This book leaves no stone unturned and we are led through a very complex world starting with defining the term ESG, what it means to different industries and how to leverage the diverse data sources needed to measure and implement a strategic investment. A must read for every Head of ESG Investing officer looking to quickly master the subject to maximize their returns."*—**Bartt Kellerman, Founder and CEO of Battle of the Quants Worldwide**

*"Many executives do not understand what makes their organization sustainable, even as it undergoes the process of Digital Transformation. They don't understand, for example, that sustainability is not some kind of CSR or philanthropy, but is an integral part of the digitalization of their company. Cristina and Diana have done a fantastic—and necessary—job of defining ESG and Sustainability, and several of the other acronyms that make up this ambiguous and complex landscape. This timely book provides an understanding of the evolution of sustainability and the many dimensions that need to be managed in order to grow healthy organizations that engage all stakeholders."*—**Jowita Michalska, CEO, Digital University**

*"This book is a blessing for those of us who need to demystify, understand, and attempt to reconcile the different lenses, metrics and frameworks that are used by different organizational stakeholders in defining and executing ESG initiatives. Unlike the CSR movement that preceded it, ESG is more than a checkbox. It takes the idea of sustainability and empowerment to new levels to be used as tools for profound and positive socio-organizational change. That said, it is a complex space, and there are many data points that can be interpreted, measured and implemented in different—and sometimes nonaligned—ways. As we fully enter the 21st century, it is increasingly crucial for students, entrepreneurs and executives to understand and codify what various ESG terms mean and what is required to integrate sustainable*

*practices into the DNA of organizations. Cristina and Diana have done an excellent job defining and vectoring the ESG landscape through a variety of lenses, providing real-world help in advancing organizational insight and clarity, for a more human-centric future.*"—**Rik Willard, Founder and Managing Director, Agentic Group LLC**

"*Cristina and Diana's book is a must read primer on sustainability that succinctly breaks down the complexities and challenges involved today and outlines a clear roadmap for practical solutions for both practitioners and academia. I would highly recommend it to both students and corporate professionals who want to prepare and be ready for the future so they can improve their chances of success significantly!!!*"—**Sanjay Sachdev, Chairman, ZyFin Holdings and Former President and Chief Executive Officer, Tata Asset Management**

"*As climate change, corporate sustainability, ESG and impact investing grow in popularity, it is important to understand what these terms mean and what is required to integrate sustainability into the DNA of organizations. Cristina and Diana have done a fantastic job defining the landscape through a variety of different lenses to provide clarity into this critical field which is interpreted in many different ways.*"—**Philip Moscoso, Professor and Associate Dean for Executive Education at IESE Business School**

"*The COVID crisis was a big test for corporate sustainability. This is a complex space, there are many contributing factors and data points that can be interpreted, measured and implemented differently. Cristina and Diana's book offers clarity to help students, entrepreneurs and executives understand the evolution of sustainability, ESG and impact investment and the different lenses, metrics and frameworks that are used by different organizational stakeholders.*"—**K. Ozgur Demirtas, Chair Professor of Finance School of Management, Sabanci University**

"*The general rule has always been 'if you can't measure, you can't manage!' The authors make a significant contribution to the discussion of how companies might more accurately and successfully measure and manage company performance toward socially sustainable results. They also make a contribution to the idea of minimizing unnecessary noise and friction through getting social responsibility stakeholders all on the same page (i.e. towards GAAP for sustainable performance as part of a more transparent process)! Kudos to the authors."*—**Charles Schott, Chief Innovation and Growth Officer of give4me; Former Deputy Assistant Secretary of the U.S. Treasury for International Trade and Investment Policy; and Former Chief of Staff at the Federal Communications Commission (FCC)**

*"In a world of continuous political chasm and ubiquitous pseudo-moralism, this book is an empirical and refreshing perspective that offers both a historical and practical analysis of all things ESG. Loved it!"*—**Frances Newton Stacy, Director of Portfolio Strategy at Optimal Capital**

*"Digital transformation is not just on the horizon, it has arrived. Strong governance is critical to the vitality and success of businesses—especially in innovative fields. This book illustrates vividly how broader aspects of ESG stem from governance. The book provides a powerful toolkit for innovative metrics for the future of governance, with clear understanding of its components and implications. Great resource for any growing company seeking to be competitive in today's changing business landscape."*—**Jeff Bandman, Expert Panel of the EU Blockchain Observatory and Forum and Principal at Bandman Advisors**

*"As we collectively evolve from asking 'Whether' or 'Why?' to 'How we address ESG' in our daily lives and financial portfolios, Transparency in ESG and the Circular Economy: Capturing Opportunities through Data provides the blueprint. Essential reading for anyone who wants to be on the right of history and the smart side of investing."*—**John D'Agostino, CEO at Dagger Consulting LLC**

*"No organization can deliver on the promise of innovation without also maintaining strong business practices focused on sustainability. The financial system in particular needs to move at pace with digital transformation*

*built on these sustainable practices. This book presents the importance of governance, coupled with emerging technologies like blockchain, in improving transparency and trust, giving firms a sustainable blueprint for successful long term, and long lasting, innovation."*—**Todd McDonald, Co-Founder, R3**

*"For the first time in human history, the world has become so wealthy that a significant number of investors can ask 'How can I ensure that my investments are having a positive effect on the causes that I care about?' Dolan and Barrero Zalles show that we're still in the early days of giving investors the information that they need to make informed decisions. This book is a comprehensive guide to the tools that we do have and gives us a preview of what we need."*—**Philip Greenspun, PhD, serial entrepreneur, and investor**

*"Sustainable investing and ESG have become popular terms, yet few people really understand all the components that contribute to the Environmental, Social and Governance metrics that are used by investors or the reporting companies. Cristina and Diana offer a detailed analysis and history of sustainability to provide the level of understanding that every entrepreneur should have to build 'sustainability-native' companies."*—**Michael Flannery, CEO Founder, Grit VC**

*"The growing demand for impact investing and sustainability requires an understanding of what sustainability risks are. Cristina and Diana have done a great job providing a foundation that makes it possible to understand this evolving landscape that is filled with so many acronyms and different approaches. Readers will have a chance to understand different types of data utilized by the various methodologies and frameworks that are used today."*—**Soner Canko (PhD), Former CEO of BKM (Bankalararası Kart Merkezi), the Interbank Credit Card Center in Turkey**

*"Bottom line, we are all called to be Environmental, Social and Governance (ESG) investors. I challenge my university students to, (1) see the dots, (2) understand the dots, and then (3) connect the dots. This simple progression is extraordinarily difficult to implement. Data may be manipulated leading to erroneous conclusions. A process for making better ESG decisions is necessary.*

*The potential for artificial intelligence and blockchain technology to confirm better results must be explored. Start with this book."*—**Mark O. Hubbard, Adjunct Professor, Mendoza School of Business, University of Notre Dame**

*"Cybersecurity is one of the most critical risks to the sustainability of organizations, governments and society. Unfortunately, cyber risks are complex and difficult to understand and often underestimated with respect to the impact on the resilience and sustainability of organizations. In a world that is becoming more reliant on data and technology, it is more critical than ever to understand sustainability and all the risk factors. Organizations are undergoing digital transformations to remain competitive, yet at the same time they are increasing their ESG (Environment, Social and Governance) risks. Cybersecurity could impact the sustainability of an organization faster and more dramatically than almost any other ESG risk. Cristina and Diana's book offers an appreciation for the history along with a holistic view on sustainability risks that make up ESG which includes cyber risk management of traditional and digital native organizations."*—**Peter Kolarov, CEO, Crayonic**

*"This is an important book that, with a user-friendly narrative, brings clarity to the many acronyms and organizations that make up sustainability. Having worked in this space for over 3 decades, I have witnessed sustainability evolve into one of the most discussed topics of our era. And critical. Any student looking to get a flavor for the risks, and in contrast, the opportunities won in sustainable organizations could do well by starting with this book."* —**Christopher Gleadle, CEO, Sustainable Viability**

*"Amidst the increased focus on sustainability, including strong values placed on human capital and life as a whole across ecosystems, companies and stakeholders alike now sit in a position to take action, or otherwise witness the consequences of inaction. For many, inaction is not an option, having taken meaningful steps to create systematic change that brings cultures and communities together over common goals. In the world defined as the Covid-19-era and other looming global threats, this book presents a manifesto of sorts on the evolution*

*of sustainability, perceptions on known and unknown facts, and the relevance of reliable data for today's marketplace. Besides, from a media perspective in particular, the information we consume is closely tethered with the data we consume, bringing accountability to a new light across the full ESG spectrum of activity.*"—**Jea Edman, CEO, Johnson Edman Advertising, Inc.**

*"The world has abruptly changed. The increased focus on sustainability to understand the impact that companies have on its stakeholders, and the environment or how external risks can affect the continuity of organizations has never been more critical than in this post COVID world. This book is an incredible starting point to understand and provide clarity around the metrics and data that are used to evaluate Environmental, Social and Governance practices.*"—**Andreu Veà, PhD, Internet Pioneer, CovidWarriors Founder and President**

*"The Coronavirus has been a driver in the increased interest in sustainability with record inflows of investment and high levels of performance due to the reduced risk. It is a complex field with many acronyms and analytical frameworks focusing on different aspects of environmental, social and governance. Understanding the many complex components that enable organizations to be resilient and sustainable is just the first step. This book is a great starting point to understand the history and metrics that are evolving into the most critical science for the future of our planet.*"—**Habib Haddad, Managing Partner, E14 Fund, the MIT Media Lab-affiliated venture fund**

*"This amazing work by Cristina and Diana put education and awareness at the forefront of ESG integration & Sustainability intersecting with digital transformation to uniquely create actionable knowledge. As consumers become stakeholders and stakeholders become consumers in organizations that they believe in and trust, loyalty to brands will be tested. Those organizations that are authentic and have true DNA to sustainability will be rewarded with consumer loyalty and valuation expansion and others that masquerade will be exposed and will experience impairment to values and cost of capital and an evaporating base. Now that we can measure externalities and meta*

*tag these newer data sets, our ability to parse with clean data structures enormously opens the ability to integrate ESG, sustainability and climate risk into our financial markets for transparency, accountability and ROI."*
—**Vince Molinari, Founder and CEO at FINTECH.TV**

*"The pandemic tested the resilience of many organizations and their connected communities. Understanding the components that make organizations sustainable has become more important than ever. In our connected world where companies engage with a wide variety of stakeholders, there are many interdependent components that need to be understood. This book offers readers an understanding of ESG and all the complex vectors involved in defining the relevant metrics to measure success. Cristina and Diana provide a strong foundation that contextually defines that wide spectrum of lenses that are used today."*—**Catherine Barba Chiaramonti, serial entrepreneur, seed stage investor, Independent Director at Group Renault, former President at French Tech New York**

*"The COVID pandemic has raised awareness about the importance of healthcare. We are learning that our prevention and management capabilities must be improved if we are to deal with similar events in the future. This reinforces the importance of developing the right ESG and the need of a more complete engagement by all stakeholders in order to provide better outcomes, especially in healthcare. ESG is complex, and there are many vectors involved in achieving sustainable ecosystems. Managing sustainability requires data, metrics and understanding. This book offers anyone interested in learning about sustainability a framework by which to understand this important yet complex space."*—**Javier Colàs, Co-Founder and CEO of Additum.es, retired CEO Medtronic Europe**

*"As cyber exposure continues to become a systemic threat to the global 10252016economy, business leaders, shareholders and regulators expect transparency towards understanding how an organization and its board are governing cyber risk. The Securities and Exchange Commission released guidance in 2018 to assist public companies in preparing disclosures about cybersecurity risks and incidents. To address these heightened expectations,*

*companies need to understand the financial and business impact associated with cyber event risk as part of their ESG oversight efforts. This book offers readers a starting point for understanding and managing this systemic risk on all stakeholders."*—**Chris Hetner, former Senior Cybersecurity Advisor to the Chair of the U.S. Securities and Exchange Commission, former Head of Cybersecurity for the Office of Compliance Inspections and Examination at the SEC, former representative on behalf of the Chair of the SEC as a senior member of the U.S. Department of the Treasury Financial Banking Information Infrastructure Committee, Expert Advisor to the Institute for Defense Analyses (U.S. Department of the Treasury), Special Advisor for Cyber Risk for the NACD, and National Board Member of the Society of Hispanic Professional Engineers**

*"The recent pandemic, financial crisis and all environmental disasters that have occurred over the past decades have drawn attention to the critical need for ESG data and metrics. We live in a highly connected world, and the sustainability of organizations impacts more than direct stakeholders, it can impact the livelihood of communities for generations. Cristina and Diana have done a great job in providing clarity with a comprehensive and easy to read description of the history, present and future outlook of ESG, illustrating it at the end with relevant examples in organizations today. This book establishes a strong foundation for anyone interested in understanding or playing a role in this critical space."*—**Miguel Palacios, Professor of Management, Madrid Campus Associate Dean of Executive Education and Research Center of Energy Director, ESCP Business School**

# Foreword

I've presented at blockchain events to the MIT and Yale communities. These were organized by the authors. Diana and I first connected over a conversation about regulation and innovation at a summer rooftop venue in New York City. I had just spoken to the crowd about how the ICO hype at the time was ignoring securities regulations. This was months before SEC Chair Jay Clayton famously testified in the U.S. Senate that he had not yet seen an ICO that he didn't think was a securities offering. We followed up about my role bringing the JOBS Act to fruition, and also how the impact of my years knocking on doors in Washington had created a large number of businesses and initiatives that were helping small companies to attain funding. Having worked in development finance in Washington, Diana was well aware of the importance of government and the need for access to capital and adequate corporate governance.

My father was a Yale alum—undergrad and law school—and I gladly accepted Diana's invitation to give a keynote at a conference she was putting together on campus. She was starting a blockchain discussion forum at the university, curating a meaningful conversation on the technology. Her vision was to ground it in reality, rather than add to the hype. She brought me on as the capital markets luminary, to help underscore that access to financing drives innovation, social impact, national security, and competitiveness in a global economy.

Not long after that, Diana introduced me to Cristina, who was putting together the flagship MIT Enterprise Forum blockchain event in New York City, and I gladly accepted her invitation to speak once again. Cristina and I caught up over breakfast leading up to the event, and I was blown away by her story—a former Team USA athlete, MIT engineer, who had cofounded an early Internet startup and taken it public. We immediately clicked over the startup capital raising issue. As former Vice Chairman of the NASDAQ, who previously oversaw the execution of over 500 IPOs at a major investment bank, I particularly appreciated her journey with the very successful IPO she undertook.

The MIT event was a major success as well—we discussed managing risk in the context of transforming market infrastructure, and the systemic loss of securities distribution from Wall Street that smaller companies depended on to both take them public and support them in the aftermarket. There is ample evidence that the loss of the economic model that supported middle-market investment banks—caused by regulatorily mandated changes to market structure—has undermined U.S. competitiveness. These investment banks were once essential and active intermediaries that raised capital to fund innovation, underwrote small IPOs to drive earlier exits, and supported these companies in the aftermarket. Any steps to fix the underlying issues and bring capital to companies will have a great effect on improving our economic competitiveness.

Over the years, I have worked with leaders in AI and many other emerging technologies at their early stages. I realized Cristina is someone who has been at the cusp of major market trends and has an eye for detecting systemic problems in need of solutions well before most anyone. It is not for no reason that this book came about. In the context of increasingly privately held companies, alongside digitization across industries, the ESG movement is emerging as a strategic issue at the core of long-term business prospects. Cristina's data expertise and Diana's development finance experience make the perfect combination to discuss this trend, especially in light of disruptive emerging technologies such as blockchain.

From the standpoint of capital raising, ESG impact is increasingly a key factor that will determine companies' eligibility to attract capital from the massive wave of sustainability-minded funds. Yet, managing and interpreting the data behind ESG is a major challenge—especially given that there are a wide variety of ESG criteria in use—that poses challenges to management teams and may hinder their ability to attract funding. Getting this right will greatly facilitate bringing capital into the hands of entrepreneurs and unlocking the benefits that I have long advocated for. This book rightly identifies the challenges to forming an integrated view of the full ESG impact of corporate activity, and the role that emerging technologies will play in lending clarity to confront these challenges.

In the face of tangible global challenges, ESG is not a fad. It is a major trend that is gathering momentum. It will drive capital allocations, regulatory developments, and corporate activity well into the future. With the Biden administration causing the United States to rejoin the Paris Climate Agreement, there is no doubt that executive action and legislation will combine to accelerate the use of ESG.

ESG is becoming a core component of business strategy. The authors clearly illustrate the role of businesses, in an increasingly connected world, as stewards of the environment and of society, while highlighting the reasons behind the wave of popular interest in ESG. I have borne witness, in my years since acting as Vice Chairman of the NASDAQ, of the dramatic increase in sustainability-minded market activity, driven by the growing consensus that ESG is a core principle that will be used to mitigate risks that otherwise might greatly damage companies' viability.

For example, with digitization across sectors, particularly disinterme-diating centralized parties, as in the case of financial innovations, cyber-crime has risen as a major threat to society as a whole. I'm particularly wary of this issue, as I have built and currently manage a fully decen-tralized investment bank. I have also been involved with a number of blockchain-related exchanges, ATSs, and platforms (INX, KoreConX, 55.com, Templum) aimed at reducing transaction costs to benefit trans-fers of intangible goods and frequency of distribution. Yet, without adequate compliance systems in decentralized infrastructures, bad actors can utilize digital platforms to finance and participate in illicit activities. In crypto trading platforms, I heard from a U.S. government official of one instance where more than $1 billion worth of illicit funds was trans-ferred from Venezuela to Switzerland. There was no clear indication of who was behind this transfer. Understandably, it triggered indigestion with some on Capitol Hill.

This book is a timely discussion for two reasons. First, it presents a strategy and roadmap for how companies can become eligible to attract the massive financial flows allocated to ESG interests while remaining regulatorily compliant. Second, it introduces the concept of ESG-native startups that have embedded the relevant components of ESG into their core business strategy with a long-term view of sustainability. It makes a strong case that ESG may be required to support sustained innovation, and the underlying role of emerging technologies, including blockchain, to provide high fidelity information flows.

—David Weild IV, Chairman & CEO of Weild & Co
Former NASDAQ Vice Chairman
"Father" of the JOBS Act

# Preface

In order to create change, it is crucial to understand the underlying problem. In order to understand the problem, it is crucial to measure it. Thus, only with adequate data can one adequately report, monitor, and manage an issue so as to create a lasting change. Otherwise, it is impossible to successfully manage what we can't measure, and even less to gain insights on the results of the changes implemented, which serve to enter into a feedback loop for iteration and constant improvement.

As environmental, social, and governance (ESG) becomes a central component of investment processes, the quality of the underlying data is fundamental in order to give it meaning. Today, companies have acquired a central status in society as the source and backbone of much of human civilization. Each industrial revolution in history has increasingly heightened the role of corporations, around which human existence has come to rely on in countless ways. With status comes responsibility, and today, we experience and even take for granted that the largest multinational companies have attained a size and role in people's lives that is more extensive than the gross domestic product (GDP) of entire nations.

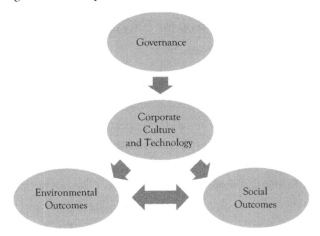

*Figure P.1  Interrelation between ESG components*

© 2022 Cristina Dolan and Diana Barrero Zalles

The wake of numerous ESG scandals for irresponsible behavior with respect to the environment, labor, society, and today's particular concerns with cybersecurity risks, have often led to the demise of entire companies. The importance of ESG has thus risen as a source of *checks and balances* for corporations and has been a topic of increasing focus. As opposed to the short-term quarterly focus of most public companies, ESG requires a long-term view that will guarantee the sustainability and mere existence of critical organizations over time. It also requires partnerships and active engagement across stakeholders.

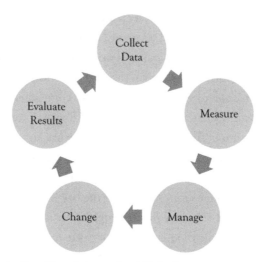

**Figure P.2  Feedback loop for ESG data**

© 2022 Cristina Dolan and Diana Barrero Zalles

ESG, however, is complex and not easy to measure, and there have been numerous approaches to standardize metrics that often led to fragmented perspectives. These varied perspectives ultimately make ESG investments difficult to compare as *apples to apples* across the board. ESG comes from governance and emanates across an entire corporate culture in order to translate into an implementation plan in practice that can effect change. This book proposes that emerging technologies including IOT, blockchain, AI, and Machine Learning can serve to organize the underlying ESG data and add transparency, in order to provide accountability and a holistic view of the full ESG impact of an operation. It is not a *how to* manual, but a discussion on the *why* and the *what* of the matter.

# Acknowledgments

It is with a deep sense of gratitude that we want to recognize the invaluable support and contributions to all those who have made this book possible, guiding us through this fascinating journey of publishing our first book. It means so much more than what words alone can convey, and we hope that the outcome of this book can speak to the significance of your contributions.

First and foremost, we want to thank our publisher BEP for making this dream come true and providing us with all the resources and encouragement to take this from an idea into a reality. To Scott and all the team at BEP, and our agent who made the initial introduction, thank you! We immensely appreciate the timely responses to all our questions as we tied all the loose ends and iterated the manuscript into the final product, the editor feedback, especially through the early drafts, which added clarity, and the efforts from the marketing team. We came to rely greatly on the overall kindness and excitement that the entire BEP team displayed throughout the process! It made an incredible difference, as you were all a pleasure to work with.

To our readers, who provided us with brilliant insights that we took into account throughout the writing process, thank you! Your inputs provided us with direction and pointed out our blind spots, helping us to fine-tune our manuscript and add substance to the discussion. The quotes you also provided us are a testament not only of the importance of the topic we bring forth through this book, but also to your faith in our efforts to bring light to it from a perspective that we believe is just in its beginnings. Thanks to all of you [names]

And with heartfelt gratitude, we acknowledge David Weild IV, our foreword writer. You have been an immense inspiration to us from even before we envisioned this book. Your diligent efforts to bring funding to areas of the economy that need it most for the sake of innovation and competitiveness speak to your integrity and insight. Your persistence in pushing forward the JOBS Act, and pioneering a decentralized model to provide startups with funding, is truly merit-worthy, and we will always be honored by the fact that you support our work the way you do.

The technology and ESG communities as a whole also deserve our sincere gratitude, for motivating and challenging us with the global, complex, and interdisciplinary issues being tackled. The rapid and much needed developments, and the brilliant minds you represent, are always a source of motivation that prompt us to deliver relevant content in the form of this book.

Finally, to our families, friends and loved ones, and everyone who back us always, your unwavering support kept us going and will continue to do so throughout this exciting path forward. We thank God for bringing each and every one of you into our lives, as you helped open the right doors to make this possible, thank you!

—Cristina and Diana

# CHAPTER 1

# History of Sustainability

## The Rise of the Company and Early Notions of Social Responsibility

### Industrialists and Philanthropy

The concept of environmental, social, and governance (ESG) arose over time in the context of business with the evolving role of commercial activity for human society and economic development.

The first industrial revolution in the late 1700s brought a shift in human society and the global economy, from being agriculturally centered to becoming urbanized and dependent on industry growth. Mechanization increased productivity, powered by energy consumption that initially relied on massive amounts of coal extraction. The steam engine was an instrumental invention that enabled physical connectivity, accelerating manufacturing by facilitating the sourcing of inputs for newly expanding businesses to produce their final outputs and sell them across different markets.

The second industrial revolution a century later, arguably the most important, built on these developments and introduced major technological advances that further improved the efficiency levels for businesses and radically transformed human lifestyle. Energy consumption came to rely on electricity, gas, and oil, while the internal combustion engine perfected the initial capacities of the steam engine. There was a massive demand for steel and chemical synthesis to produce the ideal materials to support business expansion in many forms. Innovations like the automobile, airplane, telegraph, and telephone came into existence for the first time, enabling solutions that were previously unfathomable. Later developments only continued to improve upon these innovations, arguably with decreasing marginal benefits. Connectivity established the beginning of networked ecosystems whose value derived from having a widespread community of users.

In this context, the private corporation attained an unprecedented role as generator of wealth and source of income. It became the fundamental engine behind increased productivity, innovation, and ultimately economic growth, around which much of human existence came to rely. Companies were becoming vital pillars of society by providing jobs and more cost-effective manufactured products accessible to wider populations.

Along with the wealth creation of early corporations in the industrializing world, modern philanthropy also emerged in the late 1800s. When the first industrial revolution began to draw attention on the working conditions in factories, industrialists like Andrew Carnegie and John D. Rockefeller began to donate hundreds of millions of U.S. dollars toward education, science, and other humanitarian causes. John H. Patterson, founder of the National Cash Register (NCR), led efforts to improve employee welfare in factories, which he recognized would improve productivity. Thus, the Gilded Age in the United States, from 1870 to 1900, was a period of rapid economic growth largely fueled by corporate expansion. It was also the context in which welfare capitalism developed, as a form of capitalism that included social welfare policies.[1]

The realization that focusing only on profit-seeking practices had human costs that ultimately hindered corporate efficiency led to a notion of corporate responsibility. Corporations adopted these practices on an ad hoc basis, as a strategy to prevent labor activism, unionization, and excessive regulation of workplaces. In the United States, a distinct form of corporate paternalism emerged at the turn of the century, with major corporations providing housing and other benefits to their workers in order to prevent labor strikes. The Pullman Company, a Chicago-based railcar producer, built the first planned industrial neighborhood for its workers in 1880, including housing, schools, and shopping centers. When corporate interests still persisted in other aspects of workers' lives through

---

[1] The beginnings of welfare capitalism can be traced to the early 19th century in Britain, and shortly, other European countries like France and Germany, where manufacturers began to provide new benefits to employees.

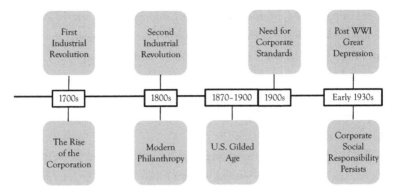

*Figure 1.1  Timeline of early notions of CSR*

© 2022 Cristina Dolan & Diana Barrero Zalles

these programs, however, worker dissatisfaction ensued. Hence, corporate paternalism didn't fully prevent strikes or unionization. Nevertheless, by the early 1900s, as corporations grew to become a significant part of the fabric of societies, the need to develop corporate standards aligned with societal values became increasingly apparent.

### Transition Toward Corporate Social Responsibility (CSR)

Post-War Period

In the aftermath of the World War I and the decline of heavy industry that preceded the Great Depression, the notion of corporate social responsibility (CSR) persisted nevertheless. American corporations were the first to use positive publicity around their personnel policies, positioning themselves publicly as responsible employers, as a strategy to manage the controversies around the war and labor. With the following economic recovery and resurgence of factory work in the advent of World War II, companies in the United States continued to take on social responsibilities. This practice eventually spread globally as well.

During the 1950s, the post-World War II tensions of the Cold War further motivated U.S. corporations to align with the needs of society in order to uphold the notion of a free society. In the meantime, the newly formed United Nations as an intergovernmental organization to maintain international peace and friendly relations among nations, the World Bank Group, and a series of development finance organizations that took shape since the 1944 Bretton Woods Agreement, raised the purpose of allocating funds with the goal of reducing poverty and improving stability in the post-war global economic system. These, however, were not private corporations and slowly came to allocate a small percentage of funds to private sector investments.

In 1953, Howard Bowen, often known as the "Father of Corporate Social Responsibility," published the book titled *Social Responsibilities of Businessman*, which officially coined the term and launched the modern era of CSR. While there had been several prior academic journals, books, and other publications that alluded to the new role of corporate leaders as companies became powerful players in society, Bowen was the first to document the comprehensive fundamental responsibilities and moral standards that executives should exhibit toward stakeholders and society, in the spirit of the existing legal and regulatory framework.

Yet, it took several decades for this idea to take off and become widespread. The 1960s were marked by a series of rebellions and social movements, including the Civil Rights Movement, followed by the anti-war protests of the 1970s as the Vietnam War brought an unwanted toll on American society after the experiences of World Wars I and II. This unrest put significant pressure on corporations as the anti-establishment era unfolded, and with it, the advancing notion of CSR. Responsibilities of businesses were called for on a proportionate basis with their social power. Firms were called to take a role in the public interest in the realm of politics, social welfare, and education and well-being of their employees.

The Committee for Economic Development,[2] with its track record since the post-war period of engaging business leadership to confront global issues and shape public policy, published the *Social Responsibilities*

---

[2] www.ced.org/about/history. The CED was launched in 1942 to benefit all Americans and promote sustainable growth. Contributions include: The Marshall Plan, Bretton Woods Agreement, The Employment Act of 1946, Pre-K Education Importance and Funding, The Bipartisan Campaign Reform Act, and Corporate Governance Report.

*of Business Corporations*[3] in 1971. It presented the idea of a *social contract* between business and society, where corporations exist as a result of public consent. Thus, society grants businesses an implicit *license to operate* inherent to their economic engagement, from which emerges the responsibility to contribute to society beyond products for sale. This concept marked a turning point where CSR began to take root on a much wider scale (that paved way toward its institutionalization in later decades).

The social contract proposed three main responsibilities of businesses, which are still relevant today: providing jobs and economic growth, ensuring fairness with respect to employees and customers, and becoming involved to improve the conditions of the broader community and environment where it operates. The following years came with the launch of new federal institutions in the United States, such as the Environmental Protection Agency (EPA). This came with a growing awareness that it is businesses that operate at the forefront of many economic changes, making their perspective fundamental for public policy decisions and necessary adjustments on global issues.

Carroll's Pyramid of Social Responsibility

By 1979, Archie B. Carroll's *Pyramid of Corporate Social Responsibility* marked yet another milestone, defining a simple framework for corporations to meet four social responsibilities. This pyramid's final illustration was published in 1991 with Carroll's publication "The Pyramid of Corporate Social Responsibility: Toward the Moral Management of Organizational Stakeholders."[4] The basis of Carroll's CSR pyramid is that the fundamental priority of businesses should first consist in profits,

---

[3] The CED also published "A new rational for corporate and social policy" (www.ced.org/pdf/A-New-Rationale-for-Corporate-Social-Policy.pdf) in 1970, leading up to "Social Responsibilities of Business Corporations" www.ced.org/reports/social-responsibilities-of-business-corporations in 1971.

[4] The Pyramid of Corporate Social Responsibility: Toward the Moral Management of Organizational Stakeholders, July 1991, Archie B. Carroll, University of Georgia, Pub: Business Horizons. www.researchgate.net/publication/4883660_The_Pyramid_of_Corporate_Social_Responsibility_Toward_the_Moral_Management_of_Organizational_Stakeholders

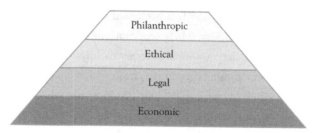

*Figure 1.2 The Pyramid of Corporate Social Responsibility by Carroll*

which ensure continued operations over time. The pyramid was accompanied by a *stakeholder responsibility matrix* for each of the four different categories of CSR, which included owners, employees, customers, suppliers, competitors, community, and the public at large.

The base was defined by the economic responsibility of businesses to be profitable, in order to return shareholder value and remain in business to provide jobs and services benefiting society. The legal layer not only required businesses to work within regulations and legal structures, but also to adhere to employment, health, and safety requirements. The ethical layer, where businesses are expected to act morally and ethically, includes several issues where definitions may not be as clear in the absence of standardized requirements and quantifiable metrics. The top of the pyramid describes the philanthropic responsibilities of organizations.

This proposal was followed by debates around the order or the categories, and commentary that it may be an overly simplistic framework. *Corporate Social Performance Revisited,* published by the University of Pittsburgh professor Donna J Wood, offered an improved framework, which took CSR metrics to a new level. The four levels of corporate responsibility defined by Carroll were linked to a three-tiered institutional framework at the legal, organizational, and individual level. Corporate actions were defined to assess, manage stakeholders, and manage implementation.

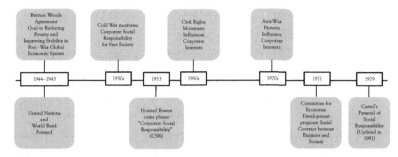

*Figure 1.3 Timeline of the transition toward CSR*

© 2022 Cristina Dolan & Diana Barrero Zalles

# Key Events That Advanced CSR Further

During the 1990s, there was an expansion in CSR practices and increased awareness at a global level. This was largely fueled by key undesirable events that further emphasized the magnitude of the adverse consequences of companies' irresponsible behavior. Thus, the responsibilities of businesses to the broader context in which they operate came into greater focus, transitioning from *nice to do* to being *necessary*. There was a realization that both environmental and social effects originated in corporate managerial decision making, and hence, governance acquired a new level of importance.

## The Oil Spill That Ignited a Movement—Launching Organizations

The Exxon Valdez Oil Spill on March 24, 1989 changed the oil industry's trajectory and called attention to the entire corporate sector by setting a precedent of the massive implications of corporate failure to adhere to its responsibilities. An oil tanker struck the Bligh Reef in Prince William Sound, west of the Alaskan shore. The resulting spill of 10.8 million gallons of crude oil in the next few days, along with the lack of proper staff, inspections, and available equipment that seriously hampered the clean-up process, made this arguably the worst oil spill in history in terms of environmental damage. The event was attributed to failed supervisory practices in terms of safety and conduct (with the captain reported to have been drinking heavily the night before and absent from the controls at the moment of the collision), fatigue or excessive workload contributing to failed vessel maneuvering, and a long-time broken collision avoidance radar, which would have indicated the impending collision.

The oil spill also ignited a transformative movement led by Joan Bavaria, together with investors and environmentalists who formed the sustainability advocacy nonprofit organization Ceres, with the objective of making CSR and sustainability the bottom line. Integrating responsible practices into core business strategies would ensure sound decision making.

### Human Rights Labor Concerns

Global awareness of labor practices was taken to a new level with human rights concerns leading to widespread protests and boycotts against companies that outsourced their operations to foreign countries where they engaged in allegedly poor working conditions such as unfair wages, unreasonable hours, and child labor. Often, these practices were commonplace in the local context of the emerging economies where these major companies set up operations, but they would not have been acceptable at company headquarters. What initially was envisioned as a cost-cutting strategy eventually led to major advocacy reactions that threatened these very businesses' bottom lines. The negative effect that these business practices posed to the local international communities where they established a presence came under close public scrutiny, with both reputational and monetary costs that forced businesses to re-evaluate their practices. Overall, the concept of solidarity with the human community has begun to establish that a business's reputation for incorruptibility can be a priceless asset. Reputation alone can mark the difference for awarding company contracts, resilience in corporate stock prices, and overall trust from the markets.

Concerns over human rights violations in labor practices in developing economies also raised global awareness, particularly in the context of outsourced labor and international operations of large corporations.

Nike, for instance, was accused of producing its footwear and apparel in Asian sweatshops with unjust factory labor conditions since the 1970s, leading to strong allegations, investigations, and a downturn in its stock price. By 2002, it began auditing its factories for occupational health and safety and eventually established a strong sustainability office with frequent reporting on metrics. In Burma, Unocal Corporation signed a contract to develop a natural gas field offshore Myanmar with the military dictatorship, known as one of the most corrupt and cruel regimes. A 1996 lawsuit filed by Myanmar residents alleged abuses such as forced labor, murder, rape, and torture in conjunction with the Myanmar military during the pipeline's construction, accusing Unocal of being complicit. Unocal agreed to compensate the plaintiffs and fund programs to improve the living conditions and protect the rights of the people living in the pipeline region. Eventually, it established a company code for international business conduct with rigorous adherence to the highest ethical standards, committing to fair treatment, a safe workplace, improving the quality of life, protecting the environment, honest communication, and being a good corporate citizen and friend of the host country.

In Africa, extractive industries such as mining often devastated vulnerable communities by forcing families to relocate in order to make way for construction sites, while subjecting local employees to abusive labor practices that put their health and well-being in peril. At the largest global mining investment conference in Cape Town in early 2020, Amnesty International called all mining companies, investors, governments, politicians, and all stakeholders to confront the human rights abuses that have taken place in the industry across the continent, where companies prioritized profits at the expense of human rights. These issues were widely reported, and eventually, resources were allocated toward responsible sourcing. Jewelry companies, for instance, have committed to responsible supply chains with respect to labor conditions.

### Climate Change

Commitments to respectful labor conditions as described are often linked to the protection of the environment. As mining companies in Africa discussed earlier violated human rights in their business practices, they did so at the expense of the environment as well. The industry's stakeholders, in their commitments to improve labor conditions, also began discussions on decarbonization and sustainability measures.

With corporations utilizing resources and producing emissions with large-scale environmental effects, their responsibility as stewards of the environment became unquestionable, as well as the pressing need for them to use resources responsibly and manage their emissions. Increasing awareness of corporate responsibilities with respect to the environment became inevitable, with visible changes in the word's ecosystems, attributed largely to corporate excesses and practices that failed to take into account the environmental impact. The magnitude of the environmental damage threatened the sustainability of the world we live in for future generations, calling into question the availability of resources to benefit from. With dramatic changes in climate in the last decades, temperature shifts, and their repercussions began a series of appalling trends that made it imperative to take action to reverse them.

The impacts of deforestation and land use have had a serious impact on biodiversity, air, and water systems. Many of the symptoms of environmental damage are seen in the oceans, which are particularly sensitive to changes in climate, with rising sea levels at an increasing and unprecedented speed. Plastic and other forms of pollution that have been dumped into ocean waters over the years have taken a toll on marine ecosystems, eventually threatening human sources of food supply. These massive changes spurred the international community to come together to address these issues. It is undeniable that we are in the warmest period on earth in thousands of years.

This degree of international cooperation across businesses and other stakeholders, for instance, was able to reverse the depletion of the ozone layer, which in the 1980s threatened the health of humans and entire natural ecosystems by significantly increasing the ultraviolet (UV) radiation levels. The 1987 United Nations Environment Programme (UNEP) Montreal Protocol drove a significant reduction in the consumption of pollutants with ozone-depleting substances (ODS), which

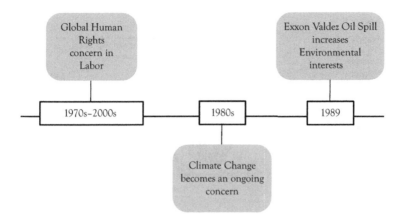

*Figure 1.4  Timeline of events advancing CSR*

© 2022 Cristina Dolan and Diana Barrero Zalles

in the European Economic Area (EEA) reduced from approximately 343,000 tons in 1986 to close to zero in 2002, where it has remained until today.

## Institutionalization of CSR

### UN Global Compact

CSR by the early 2000s had come a long way from its origins in philanthropy, anti-establishment movements, and increasing awareness. As stakeholders across sectors came to agree upon the responsibilities of corporations and the dangers of irresponsible practices, the issue of CSR became one of global concern. Due to the large scale that corporations had attained, the size of their undertakings made it only sensible for them to take up corresponding responsibilities. Eventually, a series of efforts for businesses to commit to common goals would institutionalize CSR, aiming to improve their strategic decisions and ultimately prevent massive mishaps. Global agreements, developed in close cooperation with international development organizations and endorsed by major entities around the world, contributed greatly in institutionalizing and legitimizing CSR commitments.

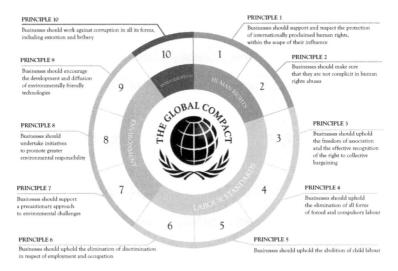

*Figure 1.5 Principles of the UN Global Compact[5]*

The UN Global Compact[6] was launched on July 26, 2000, at the UN Headquarters in New York City. This set a voluntary initiative based on CEO commitments to implement sustainability principles to focus on human rights, labor, environmental and anti-corruption practices, following a set of 10 principles. By the end of 2020, membership reached 12,084 companies in 157 countries. The UN Global Compact became a major driver of global development goals across the corporate sector, recognizing that the complexity of situations and surroundings in which corporations operate, and the complexity of the problems they aim to bring solutions to, point to various layers of particular responsibilities.

This direct targeting to CEOs forged an unprecedented link between the corporate sector and the economic development space, which would only grow stronger with further institutionalization of business responsibilities. It became evident that improving the economic situation of developing nations would be convenient for developed nations as well, such that better trade relationships may also enhance other forms of international cooperation and alignment. The concept of peace through

---

[5] Source: https://globalcompact.se/3-may-gothenburg-practical-introduction-to-the-ten-principles-of-un-global-compact/

[6] www.unglobalcompact.org

Principle 1: We will incorporate ESG issues into investment analysis and decision-making processes.
Principle 2: We will be active owners and incorporate ESG issues into our ownership policies and practices.
Principle 3: We will seek appropriate disclosure on ESG issues by the entities in which we invest.
Principle 4: We will promote acceptance and implementation of the Principles within the investment industry.
Principle 5: We will work together to enhance our effectiveness in implementing the Principles.
Principle 6: We will each report on our activities and progress towards implementing the Principles.

**Figure 1.6 PRI Principles**

commerce further highlighted the role of the corporations beyond selling products in the market, but as entities of international caliber whose decisions had a much broader impact than their internal operations.

In 2004, UN Secretary General Kofi Annan wrote to over 50 major financial institutions' CEOs, calling them to collaborate in a joint initiative with the UN Global Compact with the support of the World Bank's private investment arm the International Finance Corporation and the Swiss Government, to integrate responsible business practices into capital markets investing. The resulting report the following year, titled *Who Cares Wins*[7] made the case that embedding ESG considerations leads to good strategic business decisions that ultimately support more resilient markets and better outcomes for the broader society and economy, and thus, the term ESG was officially coined. The underlying premise made the case that in an increasingly globalized and connected world, ESG issues have become part of a business's overall management. Those businesses that perform well with respect to these issues can increase shareholder value by managing risks adequately, access new markets, and anticipate regulatory action while developing a stronger reputation as brands.

In 2005, the Principles for Responsible Investing (PRI)[8] were launched as a UN-supported network of investors committing to adhere

---

[7] www.ifc.org/wps/wcm/connect/de954acc-504f-4140-91dc-d46cf063b1ec/ WhoCaresWins_2004.pdf?MOD=AJPERES&CACHEID=ROOTWORKSP ACE-de954acc-504f-4140-91dc-d46cf063b1ec-jqeE.mD

[8] www.unpri.org/pri/about-the-pri

*Figure 1.7  UN Millennium Development Goals[9]*

to six *principles*. By 2011, the PRI had gained 1,000 signatories representing a total of $30 trillion in assets under management.

### Millennium Development Goals: First Agreed-Upon Global Milestones

With the new millennium, the global community, particularly driven by
international development organizations, agreed upon a set of eight goals
to assist the poorest nations to improve their living standards by reducing extreme poverty, hunger, and disease, and protect the environment.
All 189 United Nations Member States committed to the Millennium
Declaration that established these goals with the target date of 2015.

Global business leaders seeking a clear blueprint for ESG decision
making could take note of these concrete goals, and the UN Global Compact would facilitate much of the engagement of private corporations in
this initiative. Not only did social concerns come into play, but climate
change also came into focus in the 2000s through this framework, in support of policies and programs for corporate sustainability that evolved to
incorporate this broader mission into the business practices that defined
the global economy.

By 2015, the outcomes of the MDGs showed that while they came
to embody many policy-level decisions across governments, progress was

---

[9]  Source: www.mdgmonitor.org/outline-of-the-mdgs-notable-challenges/

*Figure 1.8 UN Sustainable Development Goals*[10]

not uniform at a global level, and there remained several gaps that were largely attributed to failed cooperation across stakeholders.[11] While much of Africa experienced remarkable changes, other developing regions, including sub-Saharan Africa, demonstrated less progress. At a global level, none of these goals was met, and the poorest and most vulnerable populations continued to be left behind.

## Sustainable Development Goals: The Shift to Align All Entities

With the lessons learned from the MDGs, the international development community reconvened to evaluate progress and a forge a revised global approach to sustainable development. The World Bank and the major regional development banks released the publication *From Billions to Trillions: Transforming Development Finance*,[13] which proposed that the only way to truly reach development goals globally would be by mobilizing resources at a much larger scale, not in the billions but in the trillions.

---

[10] Source: www.un.org/sustainabledevelopment/blog/2015/12/sustainable-development-goals-kick-off-with-start-of-new-year/

[11] www.un.org/millenniumgoals/pdf/MDG_Gap_2015_E_web.pdf.

[12] http://pubdocs.worldbank.org/en/622841485963735448/DC2015-0002-E-FinancingforDevelopment.pdf.

In turn, the only way to mobilize such capital would be to engage the private sector more closely as a major source of wealth creation for economic growth. Given that corporations already operate in complex and multi-stakeholder environments, their involvement inherently brings a wealth of different stakeholders and interested parties.

In 2015, the UN Member States unanimously adopted the Resolution 70/1,[13] "Transforming Our World: The 2030 Agenda for Sustainable Development,"[14] which defined the Sustainable Development Goals. This set of 17 goals with target date of 2030 presented much clearer and more specific indicators to measure progress for project design, monitoring, and evaluation. The premise behind this call to action, which is much broader in focus, is to involve all stakeholders in collaborating toward these goals. ESG becomes, in this sense, a reflection of an overall corporate culture that takes a broader view in its strategic decisions, with wider implications.

### Paris Agreement: Global Resolution to Confront Climate Change

There are a number of scientific models that attribute climate change to different factors, including human agency. The Paris Agreement, within the United Nations Framework Convention on Climate Change (UNFCCC), set a goal to limit the increase in average global temperature below 2°C (3.6°F) over the average pre-industrial level, hoping to significantly reduce the impacts of climate change. This requires reducing emissions, aligning financial flows accordingly, and establishing mechanisms for adaptation. Each country is obliged to determine measures, plan, and regularly report on its efforts to contain global warming. The Paris Agreement has been signed by all 196 member states of the UNFCCC as of December 2020, with 189 remaining party to it and having ratified it. The United States and Iran are the main emitters out of the countries that are not party to the agreement, although the change in administration

---

[13] www.unfpa.org/resources/transforming-our-world-2030-agenda-sustainable-development

[14] https://sustainabledevelopment.un.org/post2015/transformingourworld/publication

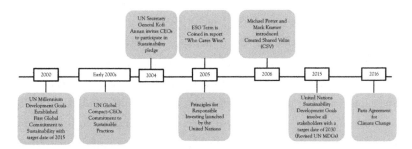

**Figure 1.9  Institutionalization of CSR**

© 2022 Cristina Dolan and Diana Barrero Zalles

in the United States for 2021 has promptly to rejoined the agreement. China, on the other hand, represents the largest country-specific market for renewable energy investing.[15] However, with a slow rate of implementation at a global level, it is expected that most countries won't meet their 2030 commitments, causing concern and significant costs.[16]

## Beyond CSR

### Shared Value as CSR 2.0

Creating shared value (CSV) was first introduced by the HBR article *Strategy & Society: The Link Between Competitive Advantage and Corporate Social Responsibility*[15] in 2006 by Michael Porter and Mark Kramer, and later further expanded upon in the 2011 HBR article by the same authors *Creating Shared Value: Redefining Capitalism and the Role of the Corporation in Society*. Porter and Kramer claim that corporations are inherently

---

[15] www.atlanticcouncil.org/blogs/new-atlanticist/climate-investing-is-it-sustainable/

[16] www.nationalgeographic.com/science/2019/11/nations-miss-paris-targets-climate-driven-weather-events-cost-billions/

[17] Strategy & Society: The Link Between Competitive Advantage and Corporate Social Responsibility, by Michael Porter and Mark Kramer, Winner of the McKinsey Award for the Best Harvard Business Review Article in 2006. https://web.archive.org/web/20130809075409/http://www.fsg.org/tabid/191/ArticleId/46/Default.aspx?srpush=true

linked to the society and context in which they operate, such that business competitiveness and the well-being of the surrounding communities are mutually dependent. The ability to capitalize on these interconnections can define a new wave of global growth where societal and economic progress advance in parallel, rather than in a zero-sum game, so as to redefine capitalism. Porter, competitive strategy expert and head of the HBS Institute for Strategy and Competitiveness, and Kramer, co-founder of the advocacy firm FSG, founded the Shared Value Initiative[18] to advance knowledge sharing on this issue. They acknowledge that the recognition of the transformative potential of the shared value concept is still in early stages and will further develop. Yet, still prominent companies like Google, Unilever, IBM, and GE have already adopted CSV principles into their business strategies.

Porter and Kramer define three ways companies can foster shared value. First, they can reconceive their products and markets, which allows them to access new markets and incorporate innovation to lower costs. Second, they can redefine productivity across value chains, which allows them to take an active stewardship role with respect to natural resources and social development, while improving inputs' quality, quantity, cost, and reliability for improved distribution. Third, companies can enable local cluster development by forging stronger ties with their surroundings in ways that can ultimately benefit them (e.g., supporting the development of reliable suppliers, infrastructure of roads and telecommunication, access to talent, and an effective legal system).

## Sustainability for Better Performance

Robert G. Eccles, Ioannis Ioannou, and George Serafeim built on this concept in a study that compared 180 U.S. companies, where half had adopted sustainability standards in 1993, to a matched sample of companies by 2009, in order to pinpoint the effects of these standards on organizational performance and processes. By 2009, High Sustainability companies, which had voluntarily adopted sustainability policies in 1993,

---

[18] www.sharedvalue.org

had distinct organizational processes in comparison to Low Sustainability companies, which had not adopted such standards at that time. [19]

High sustainability companies had developed stakeholder engagement processes with a longer-term view and organization wide incentives, including executive incentives linked to sustainability factors, and engagement with the board of directors, who were more likely to be formally responsible for sustainability. Over the long term, High Sustainability companies were found to significantly outperform Low Sustainability companies, both with respect to stock market performance and accounting measures (e.g., return-on-equity and return-on-assets). It may be concluded that the implementation of sustainability practices, and the ability to institutionalize them across an organization, is a reflection of an overall better ability to make strategic business decisions.

Yet, while many of today's largest corporations have dedicated funds toward sustainability and created CSR offices, the way corporate responsibility is implemented is key for its effectiveness as a source of business opportunity rather than merely a cost. Porter and Kramer address the tension between short-term profits and increasing demands for CSR practices by reframing the problem and presenting corporations' positioning with respect to a social *competitive context*, where long term economic and social interests are connected. They recognize that while governments, activists, and the media have come to hold companies accountable for the consequences of irresponsible behavior, social responsibility has become a priority for corporations across sectors. Rather than being a cost center or charitable deed disconnected from core business practices as earlier CSR initiatives have been, the notion of *shared value* can be a profit center and a fundamental force behind companies finding great market opportunities that also benefit society, becoming a source of innovation and competitive advantage.[20] Porter and Kramer discuss several examples

---

[19] The Impact of Corporate Sustainability on Organizational Processes and Performance, November 2014, by Robert. G. Eccles, Ioannis Ioannou and George Serafeim. www.nber.org/system/files/working_papers/w17950/w17950.pdf

[20] "CSR vs. CSV - What's the difference?" by Mark Kramer 2/18/11 https://web.archive.org/web/20130807124930/http://www.fsg.org/KnowledgeExchange/Blogs/CreatingSharedValue/PostID/66.aspx

of corporations that can analyze their social responsibility opportunities with the same frameworks that guide their core business decisions, and in doing so, have discovered unique market opportunities to capitalize on (e.g., Whole Foods, Toyota, Volvo). These are companies that have integrated ESG concerns into their very mission and vision statements, and created a corporate culture where ESG is in the very DNA of daily operations.

However, Porter and Kramer also acknowledge that CSR initiatives are often implemented in ways that can be counterproductive when they position business and society at odds with each other, ignoring their underlying interdependence. This can emphasize the costs of social responsibility and the burden of compliance as externally imposed standards. CSR implementation may also reflect a generic, rather than strategic, interpretation of the concept on the part of managers, in ways that overlook how CSR can become a competitive advantage when integrated into corporate strategy. Yet, CSV from its inception focuses on building a socially responsible value proposition within the corporate strategy, positioning it as a competitive advantage.

## The Quest for Metrics and Standardizing Environmental, Social, Governance (ESG)

### The Rise of ESG Standards

Because of the nonfinancial and qualitative nature of social responsibility, there are important challenges regarding how to standardize and streamline processes to maximize the strategic benefits and adequately measure results. This justifies the ample efforts to define metrics with the rise of ESG and forge organizational commitments to uphold them. As the MDGs and later SDGs came to become internationally agreed upon, many of these standards have drawn from the indicators they propose. ESG standard setting has taken up several forms, with a series of environmentally minded, socially minded, and industry-specific initiatives, which all developed different approaches to quantify and streamline ESG reporting and insights, and two major international standard setters with a more holistic approach toward sustainability.

In terms of environmental sustainability, the ISO 14000 (International Standard for an effective Environmental Management System framework) was developed in 1996 to minimize the adverse environmental impacts of business practices, undergoing a number of revisions over time and developing a family of standards. This standard sets the criteria for environmental management systems for companies and organizations across all sectors. It also offers a certification, having issued over 300,000 certifications in 171 countries. Later standards include the Eco Management and Audit Scheme (EMAS), which is the officially recognized environmental management scheme in the EU, launched on April 19, 2004. It was developed by the European Commission as a tool to help companies and organizations in all sectors and all regions of the world to evaluate, report, and improve their environmental impact. The Greenhouse Gas (GHG) Protocol has established global standardized frameworks for measuring and managing GHG emissions. In partnership with the World Resources Institute (WRI) and the World Business Council for Sustainable Development (WBCSD), it collaborates with governments, industry associations, NGOs, businesses, and other stakeholders and provides training for its standards and tools. More recently, the Financial Stability Board (FSB) launched the Task Force for Climate-Related Financial Disclosures, which in 2017 released recommendations to support companies disclosing this information to support capital allocation. These recommendations focus on four themes for organizational operations: governance, strategy, risk management, metrics and targets.

In terms of labor standards, OHSAS 18001 (Occupational Health and Safety Assessment Series) was introduced in 1999, focusing on occupational health and safety management. It was replaced by ISO 45001, so organizations that are OHSAS certified must migrate to the new ISO 45001 certification by March 2021. ISO 45001 has a greater focus on risk and opportunity, better alignment with other existing standards to facilitate integration, and incorporates the context of an organization. It also broadens the focus of occupational health and safety from actual employees to anyone under an organization's control, which can include the supply chain, contractors, and interns. The SA 8000 (Social Accountability standard by Social Accountability International) was introduced in 1997 by Social Accountability International (SAI), focusing on employees and working conditions, both internally for companies and at supplier organizations. It is an auditable certification that encourages socially acceptable workplace practices. The Fairtrade Mark, launched in 1997 in Bonn, Germany, provides an ethical label and stamp of approval regarding the living and working conditions of the producers of a given product. It provides an independent consumer and registered certification label for items sourced from developing countries under a fair contract for workers. The Fairtrade Mark also represents an association of international organizations to advance these interests.

The first independent organization to develop holistic ESG standards was the Global Reporting Initiative (GRI),[21] which was founded in Boston in 1997 and moved to Amsterdam in 2002. The GRI's mission is to help organizations "increase accountability and transparency in their contribution to sustainable development."[22] GRI's approach focuses on companies' impact on the broader economy, environment, and society in order to determine material ESG issues. The entire set of GRI standards[23] is offered openly and free of cost in order to drive transparency across organizations. After GRI's launch, the Coalition for Environmentally Responsible Economies[24] (CERES) and the Tellus Institute, in collaboration with the UNEP, also launched an initial draft of Sustainability Reporting Guidelines in 1999.

The Sustainability Accounting Standards Board (SASB),[25] on the other hand, represents a complementary but different approach with respect to GRI. While GRI focuses on ESG impacts on the world, SASB focuses on ESG impacts on the company. In fact, some companies report utilizing both standards. In 2011, Dr. Jean Rogers founded SASB in San Francisco, California, to improve efficiency in the financial reporting of sustainability information. These standards were announced in November 2018 and incorporated into companies' internal controls, investor communications, and public filings. Initially, SASB was focused on providing

---

[21] www.globalreporting.org
[22] www.globalreporting.org/how-to-use-the-gri-standards/
[23] www.globalreporting.org/standards/download-the-standards/
[24] www.ceres.org
[25] https://en.wikipedia.org/wiki/Sustainability_Accounting_Standards_Board

comparable data for ESG issues for the U.S Securities and Exchange Commission corporate filing standards. The goal of the organization was to provide qualitative information for investors to make decisions based on the sustainability goals within their investment thesis.

SASB has expanded its initiative to provide sustainability metrics by industry, which vary significantly based on those aspects of ESG that are most relevant, as shown by differences in business processes, geography, assets, resources and other components. For example, in order to generate economic value, manufacturing companies would utilize a different footprint than organizations with a workforce heavily reliant on knowledge workers. These classification systems offer unique industry-specific financial metrics, which are mapped to the Sustainable Industry Classification System (SICS)[26] system. Current industry categories consist of consumer goods, extracts and minerals processing, financials, food and beverage, health care, infrastructure, renewable resources and alternative energy, resource transformation, services, technology and communications, and transformation. Within each of these industry categories, there are on average 5 topics and 14 metrics, which are 79 percent qualitative. In addition, the SICS system offers additional categorizations along three factors: thematic sectors, sustainability profiles and industry classifications. Professionals can pursue a Fundamentals of Sustainable Accounting (FSA) credential, which demonstrates their knowledge of the correlation between sustainability and financial performance.

Today, these standards are utilized by major global organizations to provide transparency to investors. CEOs like Larry Fink from BlackRock have publicly endorsed SASB,[27] and many global Fortune 500 currently utilize the SASB standards and framework. SASB also collaborates with many organizations, including the *Impact Management Project*,[28] which is working toward building consensus around metrics and impacts on environmental and social issues.

---

[26]  www.sasb.org/find-your-industry/

[27]  www.blackrock.com/us/individual/larry-fink-ceo-letter

[28]  https://impactmanagementproject.com

### Initiatives Toward Alignment of Approaches

Finally, given the varied approaches to ESG metrics, their uses, the fragmentation in adoption of standards can make objective comparisons of ESG implementation difficult. Corporate Reporting Dialogue, launched at the Bloomberg Sustainable Business Summit during the World Congress of Accountants, represents a commitment toward better alignment in sustainability reporting frameworks and methods to better integrate financial and nonfinancial reporting. Corporate Reporting Dialogue is convened by the International Integrated Reporting Council (IIRC) and comprised of the Carbon Disclosure Project (CDP), the Climate Disclosure Standards Board, the Financial Accounting Standards Board (FASB), the GRI, the International Accounting Standards Board (IASB), the International Organization for Standardization, and SASB. With the Better Alignment Project, the goal is to improve dialogue and consistency among standard setters and framework developers, whose international influence on corporate reporting has become undeniable. It is widely recognized that coherent disclosures can better meet the information needs of capital markets and other stakeholders in society.

More recently, in an important move toward consolidation in ESG standards, in 2020, SASB has announced a merger with IIRC to take place by mid-2021.[29] The merger is meant to simplify ESG disclosures. Moreover, the newly formed Value Reporting Foundation will advance the initiative from SASB, IIRC, CDP charity, and the GRI to advance comprehensive reporting methodologies. Earlier in 2020, SASB and GRI announced a joint workplan to share case studies and best practices that demonstrate how both approaches can be applied together.

### Investor Demand Seeking to Profit From ESG

With the increasing demand from investors for ESG conscious investment opportunities, and the potential for significant returns, the need for portfolio construction tools and metrics to analyze and compare

---

[29] www.corporatesecretary.com/articles/esg/32356/sasb-and-iirc-merger-targets-simplified-sustainability-disclosure

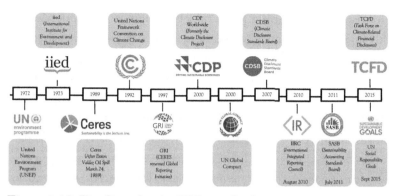

*Figure 1.10  Timeline of major ESG standard setting events*

© 2022 Cristina Dolan and Diana Barrero Zalles

investment options took off. Founded in 2009, the Global Impact Investment Network (GIIN),[30] for instance, represents a commitment to utilize ESG standards among investors. Membership spans among the largest financial institutions, asset managers, and service providers around the world. The GIIN convenes investors to enhance knowledge sharing and build tools to accelerate the development of impact investment as a field. The objective is to facilitate the allocation of capital to fund solutions that address the most pressing global needs. The GIIN has developed the tool IRIS+[31] to help investors measure and maximize the positive effects of their investments on society and the environment, taking into consideration ESG factors along with traditional financial metrics like risk and return.

Georg Kell, Founding Director of the UN Global Compact who also oversaw the launch of sister organizations such as the PRI, the Principles for Responsible Management Education (PRME), and the Sustainable Stock Exchanges, has also recognized the major demand for ESG metrics among investors. He is currently Chairman of the Board at Arabesque, a quantitative data tool that measures sustainability performance for public companies, allowing financial institutions, investors, corporations, and consultants to evaluate the alpha impact of responsible business practices. The data feeds into Arabesque's asset management firm, which uses

---

[30] https://thegiin.org/about/
[31] https://iris.thegiin.org

artificial intelligence to enhance a rules-based approach to stock selection that integrates ESG metrics with financial and momentum analyses, in order to produce risk-adjusted returns.

Furthermore, major investment data providers like Moody's, Thomson Reuters, Bloomberg, and Morningstar have also developed sophisticated ESG screening tools for investors to make financing decisions based on sustainability interests. Issues like corporate transparency in the data it provides, tracing reported data to corporate documents, accessing legal issues a company deals with, responsible practices across the supply chain, and decisions on board and executive compensation are among the factors that investors consider when evaluating ESG responsibility metrics for companies. Bloomberg has introduced ESG data with a history of over one decade, to enhance financial analysis though intangible measures beyond traditional financial valuation metrics that serve as a source of risk mitigation with respect to corporate operational decisions, HR policies and practices, and governance structures. Morningstar's Sustainalytics[32] has developed a sustainability scoring methodology and company ESG risk ratings designed to be used alongside traditional financial metrics. In a series of acquisitions that point toward some degree of consolidation, major financial data providers have also made strategic investments in ESG-focused data providers. For instance, Thomson Reuters acquired ASSET4,[33] whose scoring of extra-financial information had proven its predictive power. Its ESG scores of major financial institutions revealed significantly poor ESG performance for Bear Stearns in 2008 relative to its peers, standing near the 12th percentile of global companies. This consistently poor ESG performance had dated back since 2008 and preceded its collapse during the financial crisis. Moody's has also developed an integrated approach toward ESG as an inherent component of risk management. These trends have in turn pushed financial analysis platforms like Yahoo Finance to add sustainability scores into their basic company overviews.

---

[32] www.sustainalytics.com
[33] www.thomsonreuters.com/content/dam/openweb/documents/pdf/tr-com-financial/report/starmine-quant-research-note-on-asset4-data.pdf

# CHAPTER 2

# The Struggle to Define ESG

## Key Terms for Sustainability

ESG, although very important, is a broad concept that comes in many forms because different situations and contexts may be applicable for certain components of ESG rather than its entirety. ESG is often used interchangeably with other terms like sustainability, sustainable investing, responsible investing, impact investing, and socially responsible investing, and yet there are many facets to the various terms that have evolved in this space.

### *Corporate Social Responsibility (CSR)*

This concept refers to a company's notion of responsibility for the broader impacts of its operations. CSR has developed increasingly so as to form part of several corporations' business model and daily operations. A corporation can conduct its core business practices in ways that are meant to be socially accountable to itself, its stakeholders, and the public. CSR also refers to corporate citizenship, where companies become conscious of their impact on all areas of society such as the social, economic, and environmental effects of their business practices. CSR is a broad concept and can take on several forms, including CSR departments, philanthropy, and volunteer activities, and many ways that businesses can bring benefits to society as they boost their branding and reputation. Increasing advocacy has brought about increasing accountability for companies to develop responsible practices, their reputation, and very existence can rely on maintaining a sense of basic responsibility.

The emerging concept of creating shared value (CSV) described in Chapter 1, as a development beyond CSR, is a push to shift CSR practices from being cost centers disconnected from business strategy to becoming a source of profitability through innovation and competitive advantage.

### Triple Bottom Line

This concept refers to a company's pursuit beyond the bottom line in terms of monetary profitability, but also positive results with respect to environmental and social factors. In 1994, John Elkington, co-founder of the business consultancy SustainAbility, published the book *Cannibals with Forks: the Triple Bottom Line of 21st Century Business*, in which he identified the newly emerging cluster of non-financial considerations that would become increasingly relevant to define future market success of companies. Companies' ability to perform well across the three factors of profitability, environmental impact, and social justice would determine their competitiveness. He proposes that these should be included as factors determining a company or equity's value, coining the phrase *triple bottom line*, referring to the financial, environmental, and social elements included in the new calculation. He also discusses seven *sustainable* revolutions that reveal the evolution of issues that business leaders must respond to while raising examples from several of the world's most renowned companies.

The triple bottom line has led to an accounting framework that includes social, environmental, and financial components. The people, or social equity bottom line, can be approached with respect to organizational needs, individual needs, and community issues. The planet or ecological/environmental bottom line can be approached with respect to a company minimizing its damage to the planet, with processes that incorporate *reduce, reuse, recycle* pillars. The triple bottom line has become recognized as a UN-standardized term that extends the conventional bottom line of financial profit to incorporate broader performance of a company. A closely related concept of the double bottom line also extends beyond financial performance by adding a second parameter in terms of positive social impact. Overall, the qualitative nature of the additional *bottom lines* implies a degree of quantification, for which there have been several approaches and a degree of controversy.

### Circular Economy

This refers to an industrial model that redefines the use of resources in a traditionally *take-make-waste* industrial model, in order to design waste and pollution out of the system. This is implemented by keeping products and materials in constant use, while regenerating natural systems of operations, often at a very localized level. Certain concepts from the circular economy can be adopted as principles underlying strategy-driven CSR and CSV practices.

### Socially Responsible Investing (SRI)

Also known as social investment, sustainable or socially conscious investment, green investment, responsible investment, or ethical investment, refers to any investment strategy that seeks both a financial return and a social or environmental impact that results in positively regarded social change. While it evolved as a concept much earlier than the ESG trends we see today, SRI focuses on the perspective of the investor, as opposed to being a general term for corporate sustainability. Some socially responsible investors encourage corporate measures to actively promote social good or environmental stewardship in many forms, and thus *do good*. Others simply avoid business practices perceived to have negative social effects, such as tobacco, fast food, gambling, fossil fuels, and so on, and thus *do no harm*. SRI is a wide-spanning concept that can take several different approaches.

Certain investment approaches inspired by religious values have come under the classification of SRI, such that the origin of this concept may trace back to the Quakers in the 1750s, which prohibited adherents from taking part in the slave trade. John Wesley, one of the founders of Methodist Church, was an early and widely spoken proponent of SRI in the 1700s, calling for his congregation not to cause any harm with their use of money, particularly industries with practices that harmed the health of workers. This concept persisted with what came to be known as *sin stock* sectors like alcohol, tobacco, gambling, sex-related industries, and weapons manufacturers, as industries not to be invested in (negative screening). SRI, however, didn't gain significant traction until the 1960s when a series of social concerns that drove heated protests also came to be incorporated into investment approaches (e.g., equality for women, civil rights, and labor issues). Vietnam War protests also put pressure on university endowment funds to pull out of investments in defense contractors. The famous photograph of a nine-year-old Vietnamese girl with her back burning with the chemical napalm caused outrage and divestment pressure against the manufacturer Dow Chemical, which was exposed as profiting from the war.

This approach toward purpose-driven investment also came to define investment approaches of pension funds and institutional investors, into projects that would benefit investors at a social level, such as better housing or medical facilities. Today, SRI involves a number of investment strategies, including capital markets and community investments (e.g., directly funding a given institution), which have shown a growing market mainly in the United States and in Europe. SRI has defined several investments in government-controlled funds, mutual funds, and exchange traded funds (ETFs). Apart from negative screening and divestment, it can also take the form of positive investment as a proactive approach to adhere to a defined purpose, or impact investing within the alternative investment space. With the rise of ESG and metrics today, much of SRI has become incorporated with ESG frameworks.

Today, Islamic finance has also developed as a particularly popular subset of socially responsible investing. It relies on Sharia law to guide businesses and individuals in making capital raising decisions, as well as defining permissible types of investments. Islamic finance traces its roots to the seventh century, and over time, early Islamic caliphates had developed more sophisticated market economies than Western Europe by the Middle Ages. Islamic finance was formalized in the late 1960s and experience further gradual development ever since. It is based on the concept of risk sharing, where an Islamic bank would pool investors' money and assume a share of profits and losses. This philosophy also revolves around eliminating exploitative interest charges. Today, there have arisen a number of profit and loss sharing contracts, as actively managed mutual funds and passive funds, which screen investments for Sharia compliance by parsing company balance sheets to determine sources of income from forbidden activities. These funds have also been included in specific indexes such as the Dow Jones Islamic Market Index and the FTSE Global Islamic Index. Other Islamic finance practices include joint purchases and leases of equity, such as home, in collaboration between an investor/buyer and a bank. Installment sales involve intermediary buyers and distributed profits. Leasing structures involve selling the right to utilize goods for a determined period of time, binding the lessor but not the lessee to purchase that good, Islamic forwards, used for very niche forms of businesses, involve prepaid prices for future sale under a number of conditions that must be met in order to render contracts valid under Sharia requirements. The complexity of these agreements may often require the need for an Islamic legal advisor.

### Environmental, Social, and Governance (ESG)

Environmental, social, and governance (ESG) can trace its origins in SRI, although it focuses on the concept of sustainability itself rather than a narrow investment approach. ESG criteria set standards for a company's operations based on how environmentally or socially conscious their operations are. Environmental criteria measure a company's level of responsibility with respect to the nature and protection of natural ecosystems. Social criteria measure a company's responsibility with respect to business ecosystems, including employees, vendors and suppliers, customers, partners, and the surrounding community. Governance criteria measure a company's level of responsibility in its leadership, executive pay, use of finances, audits, internal controls, and shareholder rights. In the last decade, major environmental concerns regarding social concerns, as well as social and corporate governance concerns that led to the demise of large firms, have led to ESG investing gaining significant traction.

ESG as a term encompasses the entirety of environmental, social, and governance issues that any company, investment, or overall concept may relate to. For specific corporations, clearly certain aspects of ESG would be relevant, while others would not, but it's still important to view ESG in its entirety. Only with a holistic approach can the connections among ESG issues be drawn and compared across different sectors in order to draw insights and make decisions. Thus, ESG is not limited to just environmentalism or just social concerns, even though only a subset

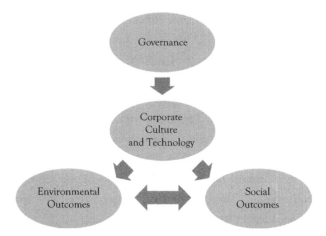

*Figure 2.1 ESG is defined by management and culture at a governance level*

© 2022 Cristina Dolan and Diana Barrero Zalles

of these may be relevant for a particular analysis. Overall, any environmentally or socially sound practices would trickle down from a company's decision-making structures, which are embedded in its governance. Therefore, ESG originates not from isolated issues of concern but from a broader awareness ingrained into the entire corporate culture that a company sets, which influences all aspects of its daily operations and core strategic principles. Leadership is key for setting a trajectory that will trickle down across an organization to define ESG implementation in various forms, integrated within the business model and strategy of a company.

## Importance of Precision

The terms that have been coined so far to define sustainability can differ widely in their approach, their focus, and the perspective of the stakeholders they may represent. Specificity and measurability are extremely important in order to measure results of sustainable business practices, as well as monitor and evaluate impact objectively over time. In implementing ESG initiatives, companies must also make sure their milestones are realistic and achievable, by appropriately focusing on the subset of ESG most relevant to their business objectives. For example, in infrastructure and architecture, there are metrics around materials to be used

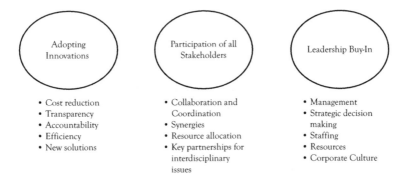

*Figure 2.2  Factors to advance ESG implementation*

© 2022 Cristina Dolan and Diana Barrero Zalles

with respect to their environmental impact, as well as considerations of carbon footprint with respect to energy usage of buildings. In the financial sector, the most relevant components of ESG revolve around governance and management's sense of responsibility, which can in turn trickle down toward fund flows directed at particular concerns with recognition of the multifaceted impacts on the economy. Technology firms, on the other hand, would largely be measuring energy consumption and the amount of physical heat caused by their operations. For those firms with a social media element, socially responsible concerns may revolve around preventing abusive language while defending freedom of speech, and at the same time safeguarding users' privacy.

## Key Factors for Implementing ESG

### Participation of Various Stakeholders

The breadth of ESG and the stakeholders it impacts inherently requires an integrated approach that actively engages all parties involved. Collaboration and coordination can produce synergies in confronting global and complex issues such as climate change and supporting small and medium enterprises across local economies. Key partnerships are crucial across the public and private sector, and particularly NGOs, which often have very specific and valuable expertise in specific fields.

## The Purpose Behind ESG: The Church and Academics

Among the various stakeholders voicing the importance of ESG, for instance, Pope Francis released a 2015 encyclical *Laudato Si: on care for our common home*,[1] where he called for a swift and unified global action toward ESG interests in light of Catholic Social Teaching.[2] There had been a history of papal encyclicals calling for a sense of stewardship over human beings and the environment since the days of the first Industrial Revolutions. In the 1891 encyclical *Rerum Novarum* ("Rights and Duties of Capital and Labor"),[3] for instance, Pope Leo XIII addressed the conditions of workers and the need for sustainable resources, stating that labor and capital must collaborate together toward common goals as the industrial age brought massive global changes in people's lifestyles. In 1991, in the wake of the fall of communism in Eastern Europe, Pope John Paul II's encyclical *Centesimus Annus* ("The Hundredth Year")[4] shed a positive light on the market economy, with the condition that capitalism shed human injustices. *Laudato Si* received particular global attention in connection with the SDGs and overall global movement toward ESG interests. Pope Francis spoke at the opening ceremony for the SDG launch at the UN General Assembly in September 2015.

He proposes that science and pragmatism cannot be in contradiction with moral questions, and we must approach global issues with an awareness of their interconnectedness among various aspects of human existence. He also denounces excessive consumerism, irresponsible economic growth, and a globalization of indifference, which have broader consequences to be concerned about that in turn threaten the economy itself by depleting the context from which it benefits. He raises the strong connection between safeguarding the environment and the safeguarding

---

[1] www.vatican.va/content/francesco/en/encyclicals/documents/papa-francesco_20150524_enciclica-laudato-si.html
[2] www.usccb.org/beliefs-and-teachings/what-we-believe/catholic-social-teaching/seven-themes-of-catholic-social-teaching
[3] www.vatican.va/content/leo-xiii/en/encyclicals/documents/hf_l-xiii_enc_15051891_rerum-novarum.html
[4] www.vatican.va/content/john-paul-ii/en/encyclicals/documents/hf_jp-ii_enc_01051991_centesimus-annus.html

poor, who are disproportionately more vulnerable to the effects of environmental degradation: "we are faced not with two separate crises, one environmental and the other social, but rather with one complex crisis which is both social and environmental." The gravity of these issues justifies the moral obligation for the global community to find a sustainable path forward. A fragmented approach toward these initiatives runs the risk of creating extremes, either protecting the environment at the expense of human concerns, or addressing social issues at the expense of the environment.

An economy that doesn't value the human person, in a consumerist society that disposes of things like it disposes people, becomes indifferent to truth, beauty, and goodness, and loses its sense of the common good. In fact, it would be the noblest use of human free will and moral agency to give up short-term interests for a greater good, as in the case of business managers who fought for justice at the expense of immediate profits, in ways that ultimately strengthened their corporate brand and reputation. This sense of responsibility, for example, pushed Johnson & Johnson to take huge losses by recalling 31 million bottles of Tylenol from shelves when a few were found laced with cyanide in 1982.

The process of writing an encyclical includes an initial period (three years for *Laudato Si*) of research and discussion with world experts, regardless of their religious or non-religious affiliation, on a specific topic of concern for a particular period in history. For *Laudato Si*, the panel of experts invited to the Vatican included Jeffrey Sachs, Director for Sustainable Development at Columbia University and former Harvard University professor of international trade. Sachs is also the President of the UN Sustainable Development Solutions Network, having advised the three past UN Secretaries-General on SDG issues. He notes that markets cannot fully function outside of a moral framework because allocating excessive profits and using resources irresponsibly create imbalances.[5] The world has witnessed the damaging effects of these imbalances through economic inequalities and environmental disruptions. From an environmental perspective, we are experiencing the effects of pollution and greenhouse gas

---

[5] www.americamagazine.org/issue/great-gift-laudato-si

emissions in a way that greatly threatens the environment and human health and well-being. In dealing with these challenges, both technology and markets need a moral direction, endorsed by leadership, for issues that would otherwise be seen as solely scientific, economic, or technical.

Financing Opportunities and Risks From Disregarding ESG: From Systemic Banks to Humanitarian Relief

As we have seen in the 2008 financial crisis, misaligned incentives arising from a principal–agent problem gave way to a context of unconstrained risk taking that ultimately led to a financial debacle. The global repercussions disproportionately affected the less wealthy, while the government bailouts and stimulus measures in response to the crisis disproportionately benefitted the wealthy. As stated by Andrew Lo,[6] professor of finance at MIT, financial crises occur when those who can't afford to lose money do so, making an existing business environment unsustainable.

Ray Dalio and the Bridgewater Associates economic research team illustrate the stark differences between the top 40 percent and bottom 60 percent of the U.S. economy and how the wealth gap has expanded significantly with overarching implications across health, education, labor, and financial well-being, which are not apparent with merely average statistics.[7] The relative conditions of the bottom 60 percent have worsened consistently, and policies have largely favored the top 40 percent. For instance, the top 40 percent has a much greater ability to save and invest in ways that create long-term benefits, whereas the bottom 60 percent survives on much shorter-term financial decisions that increase vulnerability to economic shocks. The resulting financial outcomes of both groups reflect very different realities within the same country, which also contribute to polarization. Ultimately these differences create important inefficiencies in the economy that in turn hinder productivity and output.

The total output in the world, as shown in the following table,[8] is in itself (without the potential for higher spending with higher incomes)

---

[6]  https://som.yale.edu/interview-andrew-w-lo
[7]  https://economicprinciples.org/downloads/bwam102317.pdf
[8]  www.statista.com/statistics/268750/global-gross-domestic-product-gdp/

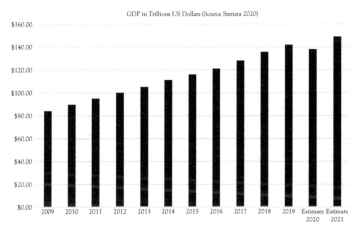

**Figure 2.3** *Gross domestic product (GDP) at current prices from 2009 to 2021 (in billions of international dollars)*

© 2022 Cristina Dolan and Diana Barrero Zalles

enough to mobilize the trillions of dollars needed to end poverty, as denoted by the indicator framework for implementation of the SDGs.[9] This global output should also provide enough resources to confront the global environmental challenges. Yet, disjointed and fragmented efforts with limited results have justified the need for all stakeholders to align and collaborate toward these common goals. In fact, SDG #17 is precisely to forge strong partnerships for the global goals.

Poverty is a scandal because it puts at stake human dignity, as described by Carolyn Woo, former dean of the Mendoza College of Business at the University of Notre Dame and former CEO of the international human-itarian agency Catholic Relief Services (CRS), who now serves on the board of Arabesque with Georg Kell. Business managers can lead in virtue in a way that trickles down across organizations into what she calls inte-gral human development. In its purely profit-seeking function, business cultivates productivity for human flourishing and mutually beneficial trade connections, while providing jobs that elevate human endeavors in all aspects of society. When we view poverty not just as a lack of resources but as an exclusion from networks of productivity and exchange, business

---

[9] https://documents-dds-ny.un.org/doc/UNDOC/GEN/N17/207/63/PDF/ N1720763.pdf?OpenElement

provides access to such networks and becomes key to reducing poverty. CRS's approach toward subsidiarity is an example of empowerment through its training to local institutions with the aim to reduce their dependence on foreign management and improve their ability to secure grant funding on their own accord. While at CRS, Woo also identified 157 development assistance projects, launched between 2014 and 2014, that utilized innovation through information and communication technologies (ICTs), becoming an early player in the larger movement of ICT for Development (ICT4D).[10]

### Leveraging Data in a Hyperconnected World to Improve Execution: Across Disciplines, From Health Care to Government to Major International Organizations

Cisco Systems, jointly with ITU, predict the frontier of ICT4D to rely on trends toward connected sensors, machine-to-machine communications, machine-to-people connectivity, and wireless sensor networks feeding into big data repositories.[11] Machine-produced data, such as that derived from sensors, and the open availability of this data, would be defining factors of this trend. The use of the Internet, in combination with mobile technologies and big data analytics for global development projects, has expanded significantly and improved outcomes. The OECD has developed an Innovation Strategy[12] to boost the effectiveness of SDG-related initiatives. It proposes a set of principles to deploy innovative technologies and measure results. It highlights the role of firms, individuals, and policy in advancing innovative solutions to overarching challenges, and the importance of knowledge sharing across all stakeholders.

In the health care space for instance, Johns Hopkins University alone has launched over 140 mHealth (mobile phone-enabled health care) projects in emerging economies. Under Dr. Alain Labrique, epidemiologist

---

[10] https://static.sched.com/hosted_files/crsict4dconference2015a/84/2015%20 ICT4D%20Conference%20Welcome%20Presentation%20Final.pdf

[11] www.itu.int/en/action/broadband/Documents/Harnessing-IoT-Global- Development.pdf

[12] www.oecd-ilibrary.org/content/publication/9789264083479-en

and founding director of the Johns Hopkins University Global mHealth Initiative, and advisor to a number of global health agencies, including the World Health Organization, UNICEF, USAID, and the mHealth Alliance, a consortium of evidence-based mHealth projects has pioneered a needs-based approach to public health in resource-limited settings where disease and mortality risks are highest.[13] Moreover, with the initial support of USAID and later the WHO and additional partners, the Digital Health Atlas,[14] which started at JHU, aims to build a central repository to register global digital health deployments. It is designed to improve transparency and reduce duplication of resources while providing useful open-source data and best practices for governments, technologists, donors, and other stakeholders to better coordinate and implement digital health initiatives.

In the public services space, the Access to Information (a2i)[15] program in Bangladesh, which forms part of the Prime Minister's Office under the Digital Bangladesh agenda, has introduced a citizen-centric public services that capitalize on citizen engagement through tech platforms. Under the direction of Anir Chowdhury, the program has pioneered the world's first innovation lab of its kind, bringing together an ecosystem of stakeholders across the country with a holistic approach to government that makes use of technology to enhance financial inclusion, civil registry, country statistics, e-services from crucial ministries, and overall cooperation. Through a Facebook page and groups, public officials can communicate with citizens at a much more real-time and localized level, in order to respond to needs more efficiently. With the widespread use of social media, damage to a rural road can be photographed and uploaded onto the page. The improved knowledge sharing can greatly enhance tailored solutions. Officers have been shown to use the platform even in late night hours to answer public queries, provide directions to subordinates, and respond immediately to private demands.[16] The open access to data and transparency has improved governance, reducing the time to response to

---

[13]  www.jhumhealth.org

[14]  https://digitalhealthatlas.org/en/-/

[15]  https://a2i.gov.bd

[16]  http://a2i.gov.bd/publication/social-media-empowering/

needs, solved a number of challenges, and reduced the costs of providing services.

Another example of an ecosystem wide initiative leveraging data and innovation is Office of Innovation at UNICEF, which cultivated a startup mentality in its organizational culture, established principles of innovation modeled after those of tech companies, which include being data-driven.[17] Apart from its Global Innovation Center, it launched an Innovation Fund with new models of investment leveraging innovations, with key founding members including the Walt Disney Company and the Government of Denmark. One key area of focus is to implement ICT in contexts of rapid urbanization, where historically, the pace of city expansion exceeded the availability of basic services—hence the emergence of slums. After a series of hackathons where solutions were piloted, including wearable devices documented in the *Wearables for Good Challenge* handbook,[18] an urbanization handbook titled *Innovating for Children in an Urbanizing World* proposes a number of use cases to deploy smart technologies to improve infrastructure (e.g., water and sanitation), transportation, basic services in health care and education, adequate response to hazards, natural disasters, and pollution, and solutions for citizen engagement and skills development to facilitate access to opportunity. [19]

Finally, the World Bank has launched an Open Data site[20] to facilitate access to data for its projects, while at the same time implementing privacy protection safeguards. It has also explored the use of non-traditional data sources and techniques to enhance the delivery of services, decision making, and citizen engagement across its investments. Moreover, it allocated a Development Data Group[21] under Haishan Fu to further the use of data for development projects across sectors and across stakeholders. Interactive storytelling and data visualizations, for instance, can greatly enhance insights collected on progress toward the SDGs, while survey

---

[17] www.unicef.org/media/59736/file/Core-commitments-for-children.pdf

[18] www.unicef.org/innovation/media/1416/file/Wearables%20for%20good.pdf

[19] www.unicef.org/innovation/media/156/file/Urbanization%20Handbook%202017.pdf

[20] https://data.worldbank.org/country/colombia

[21] www.worldbank.org/en/about/unit/unit-dec#2

data from across countries can be compiled and compared in useful ways to gather key insights. The use of big data to address the SDGs was also addressed during the Spring Meetings of the World Bank Group.[22]

Overall, the international development space has increasingly come to focus on measuring the results of each investment, incorporating measurable indicators into the design of each project and methodologies to monitor and evaluate them over time.

### The Importance of Leadership: an Ecuadorian Minister, a U.S. Presidential Candidate, and ECB President Creating Awareness and Taking Action

Leadership with integrity has become of utmost importance as a factor to ensure sustainable and responsible corporate practices. It sets the stage for corporate behavior and corporate culture, which are inherently linked, to respond to ESG concerns and adopt a sense of responsibility.

Another Arabesque board member, Yolanda Kakabadse, is also former President of the World Wildlife Fund International, former Minister of the Environment of the Republic of Ecuador, in addition to having held a number of leadership roles across various NGOs and advocacy groups and organizations.[23] Yolanda's initial role as founder of the NGO Fundación Natura in Quito, which was established as a response to local demands, brought awareness to the need for better defining environmental sustainability and educating various stakeholders at all levels. In order to contribute with solutions effectively, there is a need for awareness. Her endeavors to educate the population on issues like deforestation, land use, water pollution, emissions, and biodiversity led the Ecuadorian government to appoint her as Minister of the Environment. She contributed to devoting resources for protecting ecosystems like the oceans, which are the major source of food for a significant part of the population and yet have been used as a dumping ground.

---

[22] www.worldbank.org/en/news/feature/2018/04/27/using-big-data-to-achieve-the-sdgs

[23] https://growthlab.cid.harvard.edu/event/leadership-global-environmental-conflicts-conversation-yolanda-kakabadse

At a global level, her leadership roles in various international organizations (e.g., World Resource Institute, Earth Summit, WWF, World
Economic Forum, Inter-American Dialogue) have called for close collaboration with the financial sector to allocate resources to address conservation priorities. Kakabadse has been a thought leader helping financial
industry players reframe the value of biodiversity and the natural capital
of the environment, as opportunities for profitable investments in support of sustainability processes. She paved way to define the relevance of
financial industry players in protecting ecosystems by changing attitudes
toward these issues in ways that can see opportunity in adjusting their
model of work, benefit from tools to define ESG funding priorities, and
create excitement on the part of both funders and recipients of funding
for sustainability endeavors.

In the United States, former U.S. presidential candidate Al Gore
was very successful after his government career, adding value through
his later work in advancement of sustainability issues.[24] Like Kakabadse,
Gore found a huge need to begin by educating the public on the needs
and opportunities presented by ESG. His book *An Inconvenient Truth*
not only became an international best seller, but the movie version won
two Oscars, the audio version won a Grammy, and his overall endeavors
for climate action won him a Nobel Peace Prize in 2007. Again like
Kakabadse, Gore eventually focused on mobilizing financing toward sustainability issues, joining forces with large tech firms and becoming a
partner at the Silicon Valley venture capital firm Kleiner Perkins. Gore
also founded the advocacy group Climate Reality Project.

In running Generation Investment Management, Gore has intended
to re-envision capitalism by shifting incentives of financial and business
players toward reducing the damage of commercial excesses in the realm
of environmental, social, and political spheres. Corporate excesses are a
form of irresponsibility that he deems to be unsustainable in the long
run. It is this long-term view that more than justifies investments in sustainability, having recognized how short-term investment horizons, often
motivated by pressure to report quarterly accounting measures, have been
extremely damaging for businesses and overall economies. It is with this

---

[24] www.theatlantic.com/magazine/archive/2015/11/the-planet-saving-capital-
ism-subverting-surprisingly-lucrative-investment-secrets-of-al-gore/407857/

very approach that Generation has made more money by traditional metrics, by investing in an environmentally conscious manner, than most fund managers in pursuit of profits regardless of ESG costs.

This performance has defied the notion that individual investors are often told, that it's impossible to beat the market as a justification for passive investing. Generation's global equity fund, where most of its assets are invested, has performed consistently above the growth rate of the MSCI World Index, which represents global stock market performance. Even through the turbulent financial markets events that occurred in the period 2005 to 2015, Generation's average yearly return of 12.1 percent greatly outperformed the MSCI's average of 7 percent. It earned the rank of second place in a survey of among over 200 global equity managers, while the volatility was among the lowest. This track record earned it the recognition of major fund managers, that a long-term ESG-focused perspective may just be the opportunity the market has been missing.

Finally, ECB President Christine Lagarde has openly endorsed sustainable growth as a strategic objective for Europe. In her November 2020 keynote at the European Banking Congress,[25] sustainability is a central factor behind the trend toward digitization in order to foster adequate growth that can ensure jobs, meeting social needs, including health care and education, and addressing climate change. She acknowledges that meeting these goals requires policy actions that go beyond monetary policy but address the broader context in which central banks operate. She frames the task at hand as not attempting to foresee but to enable the future that is already upon us.

Lagarde has also set green policy as a priority for the European Central Bank (ECB) agenda, defining it as a decisive factor for bond buying.[26] The ECB's € 2.8 trillion asset purchase scheme is being used to advance environmentally friendly pursuits, analyzing the impact of all of its operations in the fight to contain climate change. This has made the ECB the first major global central bank to adopt green objectives at the center of its bond buying agenda.

---

[25] www.ecb.europa.eu/press/key/date/2020/html/ecb.sp201120~e92d92352f.en.html

[26] www.ft.com/content/f776ea60-2b84-4b72-9765-2c084bff6e32

# CHAPTER 3

# ESG Landscape and Importance Today

## ESG's Unprecedented Importance for Business

As corporations today have attained a size and scale comparable, or even larger than, entire countries, their actions have attained a level of impact that can be greater than that of entire governments, which justifies the need for checks and balances to ensure responsible behavior. Today, there is arguably an unprecedented level of pressure for companies to take ESG considerations seriously in their decisions. Not only is there a promise of better performance when ESG makes its way into core strategic considerations, but their very existence in the long term may rely on this.

From a purely bottom-line perspective, by not integrating environmental, social, and governance (ESG) into a company's business strategy and utilizing metrics, significant amounts of waste can be created, adding unnecessarily or easily reducible costs. In terms of revenue, ESG can be a competitive advantage when customer preferences revolve around sustainability of products and services consumed: a trend that is increasingly apparent among millennials and younger generations. Ultimately, ESG underlies the sustainability of companies as their ability to survive in the long term by ensuring continued good practices, sustainable operations, and adequate prevention and response to risks. It provides a framework to approach factors beyond the market, which can still represent material financial risks.

After a history of corporate excesses with global consequences, and increasing media and technology fronts to push for transparency, more stakeholders are holding businesses accountable for the consequences of their practices. Companies are increasingly held accountable for issues beyond their pure market operations. These nonmarket issues demand a nonmarket strategy that takes into account ESG.[1] Thus, market assets of a corporation, if managed irresponsibly, can become liabilities in a nonmarket sense. Eventually, firm behavior would reflect not just its market interest but its overall values, hence the importance of a well-founded corporate culture.

### ESG as a Form of Risk Mitigation

ESG scandals can severely damage a corporation's reputation and obliterate its performance in the markets, becoming a risk that companies are increasingly devoting resources to manage. The most productive ESG implementation will not only establish an adequate risk management framework to prevent and mitigate scandals but also proactively integrate ESG into the very DNA of a business model. The only way to achieve this successfully is to immerse ESG principles into the entire corporate culture, which is defined and endorsed by management and the board, and trickles down throughout all the staff to affect all aspects of business operations. There are a number of major stakeholders that have been forced to ensure corporate-level checks and balances, mostly at an ad hoc level in the absence of an overarching framework and the various different lenses with which ESG issues are viewed.

## Key Players Adding Checks and Balances to Companies

### Investors

Sustainability and ESG have become popular topics in the growing trend toward responsible investing. Investors are increasingly using ESG metrics to evaluate potential investments, even if purely from the perspective of financial gains, given the promise of higher returns. This has pressured ESG companies to be responsible with their resource allocation, strategic

---

[1] David Bach and David Bruce Allen, "What Every CEO Needs to Know about Nonmarket Strategy."

in their decisions, and transparently report the results of their operations. Investors, who provide funding and thus would have a say in company operations, demand clarity and consistency in order to evaluate portfolio creation methodologies and compare ESG-minded options as financial products across the investment horizon. Often, they are subject to commitments and milestones to produce specific returns, and below-par performance could signify the loss of an investment.

ESG metrics for companies focused on results other than financial performance can also help investors reduce the risk of massive losses from failure or scandal from investing in, further increasing the pressure for strategic resource allocation. Moreover, younger generations of investors are increasingly interested in purpose alongside returns, as seen by investment trends among millennials. There is also an increasing demand for data, which furthers the push toward transparency and accountability.

### Companies

Major corporations and small companies alike are looking to become more sustainable, not only to reduce the risks of major scandals but also to remain competitive. Companies are being held responsible for all aspects of their supply chains. External demands from the public can take the form of customers seeking responsibly made products and services, advocacy groups raising issues of concern with corporate practices to the public eye through social media and other outlets, and formal media groups reporting on any major scandals. Internal demands from employees influencing management decisions to meet their needs, as well demands from top management and board to meet ESG goals, have put pressure for companies to institutionalize corporate responsibility practices. This can be seen with the trend toward corporate social responsibility (CSR) activities across companies of all industries, and even the establishment of formal CSR departments and C-level positions focusing on sustainability. Google, for example, has been able to buy carbon credits, investing in green projects that ultimately offset its carbon footprint to zero.[2] With

---

[2] https://static.googleusercontent.com/media/www.google.com/en//green/pdfs/google-carbon-offsets.pdf

these initiatives, key drivers of success to mitigate ESG-related risks and advance competitiveness would be effective leadership based on clearly defined ESG strategies and the ability to proactively identify issues of concern to prioritize.

Holding true to their mission and vision and setting a long-term view for corporate strategy are important components that establish underlying frameworks to support a sense of responsibility. A sense of responsibility among leadership is a crucial defining factor to make ESG part of the organizational culture. Johnson & Johnson was among the first companies to establish a mission that clearly spelled out a sense of responsibility and continues to be effectively communicated to all staff to form a basis for the entire corporate culture. Forged on a plaque at the company headquarters, this *Credo*[3] was written by the founding chairman Robert Wood Johnson himself in 1943 and holds a long tradition of excellence and responsibility, acknowledging the importance of employees, customers, and the community. More recently, ESG has made its way into an increasing portion of company mission statements, whether explicitly or implicitly, and has also strengthened its branding.

### Policy and Regulation

Global policies and regulations have increasingly aligned with international commitments toward ESG interests, which have gained traction as a response to the social and environmental consequences of past irresponsible behavior, and the need for accountability and governance. In the United States, most recently Biden has vowed to rejoin the Paris Agreement, which will make environmental issues a top priority for major companies. The UK has also established an environmental and sustainability policy[4] that allocates resources and staff toward the implementation of established measures for ESG practices. Heads of state are also looking into passing laws around Ecocide, which would make it a crime to destroy nature. Multinational corporations that operate in regions with

---

[3] www.jnj.com/credo/

[4] https://assets.publishing.service.gov.uk/government/uploads/system/uploads/attachment_data/file/356348/Environmental_and_sustainability_policy.pdf

sustainability regulations are obliged to comply, giving these regulations a global nature in themselves.

The European Union (EU) has been a global leader in enacting ESG regulations,[5] making clear that sustainable development will be an utmost priority in its decisions. It presents a holistic approach to the United Nations' (UNs') 2030 Agenda for Sustainable Development across member states, with clear measures coming from the European Council and European Parliament and budget allocations toward these goals. The European Commission's 2018 action plan for financing sustainable growth[6] proposes 10 reforms in three sectors that encompass directing capital flows toward sustainable investments for inclusive growth, integrating sustainability into risk management, and fostering transparency and a long-term view for financial and economic activities. This in turn has led to the creation of an official sustainability taxonomy as a unified classification system for the region to be used to channel fund flows, disclosure of duties through regulations and directives, setting benchmarks to measure impact and progress, and establishing sustainability preferences through a consultation on the addition of ESG considerations for the Markets in Financial Instruments Directive (MiFID II) and the Insurance Distribution Directive.

The European Commission published guidelines for reporting[7] to provide clarity for funding a climate-neutral economy and implementing investments of the necessary scale. Moreover, the recommendations of both the Technical Expert Group (TEG) on sustainable finance and the Task Force on Climate-Related Financial Disclosures (TCFD), set up by the Financial Stability Board of the G20, gave way to the EU-wide Non-Financial Reporting Directive,[8] which member states are obliged

---

[5] https://ec.europa.eu/environment/sustainable-development/SDGs/implementation/index_en.htm

[6] https://ec.europa.eu/info/publications/sustainable-finance-renewed-strategy_en

[7] https://ec.europa.eu/info/publications/non-financial-reporting-guidelines_en#climate

[8] https://ec.europa.eu/info/business-economy-euro/company-reporting-and-auditing/company-reporting/non-financial-reporting_en

to transpose into their laws. The TEG has also produced a Green Bond Standard,[9] with clear criteria for issuing green bonds.

## Customers

As companies are becoming increasingly customer-centric as part of their competitive strategy, customers are increasingly demanding of sustainably made products and services. This strengthens the brand and reputation of companies with transparent supply chains that can guarantee fair labor practices and environmentally friendly operations. In an unprecedented way, customers now have a voice that can influence management decisions through their buying power. Customers are responsive to the media coverage and exposure of corporate abuses on the part of advocacy groups, which are intended to represent their interests as part of the public interest. They can collaborate with public outcry by boycotting products, which can have a massive impact on company decisions.

## International Community

With the global consensus brought about by the SDGs and the initiatives they have prompted, the international community becomes a powerful force to mobilize funds and enhances cross-sector agreements for the implementation of cross-cutting ESG initiatives.

In this context, the Republic of Seychelles, in collaboration with the World Bank, has issued the first sovereign blue bond, raising $15 million from international private investors to fund sustainable uses of marine resources.[10] The overall model includes the blue investment fund managed by the Development Bank of Seychelles, in addition to a smaller $3 million blue grants fund by the Seychelles Conservation and Climate Adaptation Trust (SeyCCAT). The fund is partially guaranteed by the World Bank and establishes eligible activities such as promotion

---

[9] https://ec.europa.eu/info/files/190618-sustainable-finance-teg-report-green-bond-standard_en

[10] www.worldbank.org/en/news/press-release/2018/10/29/seychelles-launches-worlds-first-sovereign-blue-bond

of sustainable marine practices, improving value chains, education and awareness programs, fisheries management plans, and rebuilding depleted resources.

## Advocacy

The role of advocacy groups and nongovernmental organizations (NGOs), which have leveraged social media and traditional media extremely successfully to expose issues of concern, has served to exert pressure, often in forceful ways, to hold even the largest global companies accountable for their actions. Thus, activists and NGOs have come to shape de facto rules in a sense for important components of the global economy, bringing a new level of private politics and a sense of privatized global governance to effect, a degree of checks and balances on corporations. For example, Greenpeace as a low-budget grassroots organization was able to garner support and leverage massive power against multinational companies for poor environmental practices. Its campaigns put pressure on them, with results that no other initiatives or more established entities were able to achieve.

In 2010, palm oil exports had been increasing continuously for a decade, deriving in their vast majority from Indonesia and Malaysia, while their prices as commodities, which were already lower than other vegetable oils, remained at consistently low levels. Golden Agri-Resources (GAR) managed the largest planted area in Indonesia and ranked second in the world. Greenpeace documented how the plantations were destroying the natural habitat of orangutans and organized massive protests against Nestle, using a logo analogous to KitKat chocolates, a motto phrase, and at times graphic content of people eating orangutan fingers as KitKats. What mostly increased customer awareness was the scale of the online campaign and social media coverage, which went viral very quickly with YouTube, e-mail blasts, and Facebook public forums. The 2010 campaign and boycott were successful; Nestle dropped its business relationship, and GAR committed to adhere to international standards, of which there were three applicable frameworks with different levels of transparency and obligations: Indonesian Sustainable Palm Oil, Certified Sustainable Palm Oil RSPO, and TFT for delivering responsible

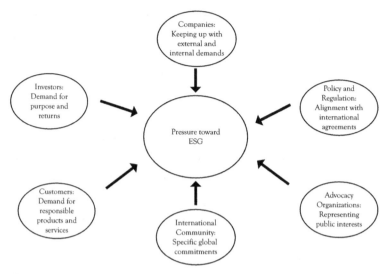

*Figure 3.1 Pressure toward ESG*

© 2022 Cristina Dolan and Diana Barrero Zalles

products. Eventually, Greenpeace even came to collaborate with GAR to publish the High Carbon Stock Forest Study, and GAR went on to launch a pilot program to investigate how to prevent deforestation.

A similar campaign in 2011 was also carried out successfully with a different subsidiary of GAR's parent company Sinar Mas, Asia Pulp and Paper (APP), which was also contributing to deforestation in its products supplied to Mattel for toy packaging. Greenpeace's strategy, which included a video of Ken being outraged by Barbie's packaging, caused public outcry such that Mattel responded by investigating the deforestation allegations and directing its packaging suppliers to stop sourcing pulp from APP during the investigations. Mattel went on to stop sourcing packaging paper derived from rainforests.[11]

A 2015 Greenpeace campaign caused Lego to end its partnership with Shell, which was exposed for Arctic drilling and the environmental destruction it caused. A campaign that included a video of toy people, animals, and an Arctic landscape built in Lego blocks and being covered in black oil brought public awareness on the issue and led to changes.

---

[11] www.greenpeace.org/usa/news/barbie-drops-rainforest-packaging/

Shell-branded Legos were no longer to be produced, and Shell eventually abandoned offshore oil drilling in the Arctic. Nevertheless, continued fracking in other states may have also made more sense for Shell financially with a declining oil price.

## Key Events Advancing ESG Interests Today

### COVID-19 Crisis

The global COVID-19 pandemic has brought an unprecedented focus on saving lives and safeguarding the livelihoods of people while reshaping markets and entire economic structures. In the months until the long-awaited herd immunity can be guaranteed, as restrictions in mobilization have affected virtually all forms of economic activity, stakeholders across disciplines have reassessed ways to organize a resilient economy for the future. With the unprecedented adoption of digital technology having reshaped work, commerce, and payments, not only can productivity be boosted, but also a less resource-dependent economy offers opportunities for economic growth to be decoupled from carbon emissions. Digitalization has maximized connectivity and access to networks of exchange for opportunities ahead.

Digitalization can also facilitate the trends to democratize access to basic services in health care and education, which can serve for the benefit of previously underserved segments of the population. While only 11 percent of U.S, consumers used telemedicine in 2019, this factor increased to 46 percent in the midst of the pandemic in 2020, with 76 percent being interested in using telemedicine in the future.[12] The telehealth industry could come to represent a quarter trillion-dollar sector in the future. The level of innovation that the COVID-19 pandemic has spurred also accelerated the development of vaccine solutions with unprecedented resource allocation and measures to ensure their safety, given the rapid pace of their development. It also put pressure on the transparency of the supply chain, given the low temperatures that the

---

[12] www.mckinsey.com/~/media/McKinsey/Industries/Healthcare%20Systems %20and%20Services/Our%20Insights/Telehealth%20A%20quarter%20 trillion%20dollar%20post%20COVID%2019%20reality/Telehealth-A-quarter-trilliondollar-post-COVID-19-reality.pdf

vaccine must be kept at while it is being transported. Many of these issues can only be effectively managed with adequate use of data gathered by connected devices.

With respect to financial inclusion, the pandemic also accelerated the development of financial technologies to facilitate not only commerce and contactless payments but also piloting financial stimulus disbursements by electronic means.[13] These innovations supported the infrastructures that can democratize access to financial services for underserved populations and unbanked communities. These underlying financial infrastructures can facilitate easier and more transparent transactions, including models for Central Bank Digital Currencies piloted across countries.[14]

Finally, the pandemic opened new avenues for online learning and training programs, in connection with teleworkable models of employment. Academic institutions underwent a period of disruption and adjustment toward online platforms. These new platforms can be fundamental for re-skilling and upskilling the current workforce to be prepared for the new employment trends in the post-COVID economy.

### Migration Crisis

Geopolitical conflicts, violence, persecution, and poverty have led to a massive migration crisis, with the highest number of refugees leaving their homes since World War II. The large numbers of displaced persons entering new countries have represented a significant financial burden for host countries when not integrated adequately into the labor force, which would make them a source of wealth creation. There is a pressing need to provide basic services and ensure citizen security among displaced populations. This presents an opportunity for ESG-minded companies to capitalize on providing solutions for migrants' integration into their host countries, particularly with respect to their productive capacity with the diversity of skills refugees bring. These may include opportunities for securing livelihoods though employment opportunities, housing needs,

---

[13] www.ecb.europa.eu/press/key/date/2020/html/ecb.sp201022~d66111be97 .en.html

[14] www.bis.org/publ/arpdf/ar2020e3.pdf

and access to financial services through innovative platforms targeting unbanked communities to improve financial inclusion. In the realm of global immigration, the global remittance market, where foreign migrants transfer funds to their home countries, was valued at $682.6 billion in 2018 and projected to grow to a size of $930.44 billion by 2026.[15] The rate of interest these transfers are charged has historically been extremely high, which has raised concerns over the need for financial solutions to better meet the needs of this market.

## Sustainable Agriculture

With population growth and limited arable land for agriculture, it has become of paramount importance to utilize resources efficiently and improve the productivity of yields. Investing in green agriculture has become a niche subset of the financial industry, with the Global AgInvesting conference gathering investors and stakeholders in this space around the world since 2009. Agribusiness overall has begun to experience the benefits of innovations that support sustainable practices such as responsible uses of water and energy, as well as transparent and fair supply chains. Apart from the varied initiatives to tackle food waste, a number of initiatives have advanced levels of productivity significantly.

In Chile, the Atacama Desert represents among the richest sources of solar energy around the world. The fruit exporter Subsole, among the top five in the country, secured financing from the Inter-American Development Bank to build a solar plant and an entirely renewable energy-powered irrigation system to produce and export grapes while lowering electricity costs.[16] Subsole thus became Chile's first fruit exporter to rely on renewable energy. This project is also a case of successful shared value operations, where resources were dedicated to ensure a competitive workforce among grape pickers. Because the company historically grows 30 percent of the grapes it exports, it relies heavily on community ties with surrounding small-scale farmers. In boosting their efficiency, including the provision of better health care services, and a gender equality

---

[15] www.alliedmarketresearch.com/remittance-market

[16] issuu.com/sabine04/docs/idb_share_value_subsole_-_english

component to provide jobs for women, it can also better facilitate their access to international markets. The shared value analysis found that the benefits of expanding access to health care at the operation would be 2.5 times higher than the costs of letting workers depend on external health care facilities, which in a rural area would represent physical distance, low reliability, and additional time away from productive employment activities.

Innovations and connected devices have given way to a new form of *vertical farming*[17] that capitalize on increasing food production using less land. Crops grown on panels of soil stacked on top of each other and provided with adequate amounts of light and water are harvested in a controlled environment that reduces the variability of weather and pests. Moreover, connected sensors can provide data to further improve productivity, efficiency, and reduce energy costs. AeroFarms, the largest indoor vertical farm in the world, has implemented a data-driven approach to farming and the ability to grow food in urban cities where increasing populations are expected to reside. Average yields are estimated by the company to be 390 times higher per square foot relative to field agriculture. The physical proximity to the market of consumers can also facilitate transparency and best practices in supply chains, with shorter distances to travel and less transportation costs and emissions. Due to costs, materials, and energy usage, while vertical farms may not be expected to replace traditional farms, they do hold promise to improve sustainable food production in the context of urbanization and population growth.

### Cybersecurity Risk

With the increased digitalization that the world has experienced to date, there is also a heightened cybersecurity risk that affects all stakeholders that form part of the connected ecosystem. While digitalization may on the one hand reduce companies' carbon footprint, it also exposes them to cybersecurity risks, which are in general much less understood across the board so as to set an effective risk mitigation strategy. Moreover, the consequences of cybersecurity breaches can be much more drastic and

---

[17] www.ey.com/en_us/purpose/next-up-mark-oshima-farming-up

immediate than environmental risks, with a dramatic impact on the social and governance side of ESG. With cybersecurity breaches, customers' data can be lost, employees can lose their jobs, shareholders are at a loss, and supply chains can be dismantled. Privacy is put at stake, not only at an individual level, but entire governments can lose control of their sensitive information, and entire organizations can suffer from significant reputational costs. Ownership of assets is compromised, which is particularly impactful given that transparency in titles of ownership is a central tenet of a thriving civilization, and overall well-being of communities is put at risk. Ultimately, the entire ecosystem in which companies operate can be destroyed with the effects of a cybersecurity breach.

For instance, phishing scenarios associated with remote working conditions and digital processes have created a significant rise in thefts related to cybersecurity breaches. Hackers can infiltrate into COVID-19 vaccine distribution channels and research labs, disrupting supply chains, financial transactions, health care delivery, and stealing data. In September of 2019, Ecuador suffered from a massive data breach in its financial system due to an unsecured server run by a marketing and analytics firm, where hackers leaked the identity and financial details of 20 million people, traceable to virtually every Ecuadorian citizen. The information was exposed and made freely available online for a certain period of time before measures were taken to remove it, but the damage and risks from the incident cannot be reversed or erased so easily. It is arguable that today health care data may be even more valuable than financial data, given the rising demand for prescription medicines such as painkillers in black markets. Today, it is easier to steal data online and profit from selling it than what in the past would have been to steal a painting from a museum and sell it.

Due to the immediate impact that cybersecurity risk can have on a company's sustainability, it is imperative for companies to take adequate protection measures immediately. While cybersecurity risk can affect both large and small companies, small and medium enterprises (SMEs) are particularly vulnerable. SMEs make up the vast majority of companies building up the global economy and are also the source of the majority of jobs. In general, they lack the resources and sophistication to protect themselves from threats like hacks and other attacks involving data breaches. SMEs that experience catastrophic data breaches are likely to go out of business within 6–12 months. Cybersecurity is likely one of the areas that ESG-minded companies can be most vulnerable, which in turn can catastrophically wipe out important progress made toward ESG objectives in support of important aspects of society and the environment. The sustainability of these companies can be made very fragile when it comes to cybersecurity risk, which represents a sophisticated and complex issue that there is yet little understanding to protect against. There is an imminent and growing need for these companies to develop and implement strategies to protect themselves from this risk. This requires adequate governance with respect to data, implementation of cyber resilience processes, and a strategy.

# CHAPTER 4

# But What Really Is ESG? The Challenges of Defining and Implementing Consistent Measures

## ESG is Broad and Difficult to Standardize

### Inconsistent Definitions, Standards, and Metrics

Because ESG overarches the most complex global problems, spans interdisciplinary issues, and deals with largely qualitative themes, it is difficult to standardize a single approach to represent it. ESG initiatives can take a wide range of forms across different contexts, needs, and stakeholders. Thus, there have emerged various different approaches to standardizing and reporting ESG results that are difficult to compare as *apples-to-apples*. While there is an ample amount of data that has been recorded and measured so far, there is not a single common format to organize it in order to gather insights.

As a result, while ESG terms are especially important for all stakeholders to understand thoroughly, it isn't always clear what they actually mean and why they are such an important component of investment criteria, especially due to the variability of reporting frameworks across industries, standards, and data providers. There have been a number of different taxonomies created, each adding yet another lens to address ESG issues. The problem of data inconsistency leads to a lack of clarity as to how to make sense of and make use of ESG metrics.

Due to these challenges in defining metrics, a lack of a standardized common format makes it difficult for investors to compare across the universe of ESG investment opportunities. From a corporate perspective, it is also difficult for firms to define what metrics to prioritize and how to report them effectively, in ways that would attract ESG investments into their projects. A firm that adheres to GRI, for instance, would have a different ESG outlook than a firm that adheres to SASB, and there may not be enough resources to adhere to both at the same time. Moreover, the indicators established by the SDGs may not completely align with other reporting requirements that a company is obliged to provide. The field of project finance is particularly complex in the diversity of stakeholders it involves, the jurisdictions whose legal requirements must be adhered to, the various different standards on the use of materials for construction, and the complexity of multi-party transactions. Companies may be faced with a number of different standards they can choose to adhere to, each with different pros and cons with respect to level of transparency, international level of acceptance, level of enforcement, and nature of requirements with respect to different components of ESG (e.g., specific restrictions on materials, community involvement component, company policy standards, diversity requirements in management or board).

### No Consensus on an Approach to Draw Insights From the Data

Companies and their management teams are left to define their own position with respect to ESG and report their sustainability goals, with little guidance on what approach is best tailored to their situation and what metrics would make them most eligible for funding. This is of utmost importance, given that ESG practices are key for a holistic and effective risk management framework. Mere adherence to policies and regulatory requirements may not be envisioned with the companies' best interests in mind, or with a view on how to incorporate ESG into strategic decision making and corporate cultures. This can risk keeping ESG practices as a cost center, as a charitable requirement with the burden of compliance, rather than a profit center and source of market opportunity and innovation. ESG as a form of compliance rather than a strategic endeavor also reduces the opportunity for companies to leverage responsible practices to strengthen their brands and reputation. Moreover, many of these metrics are self-reported, and a lack of understanding regarding ESG as a strategic opportunity can lead to a *check the box* approach that is less likely to draw strategic insights from the data collected. It may be well known that strong ESG-performing companies are also more competitive in terms of financial returns, but exactly how this takes place may still be unclear.

## Lack of Transparency and Accountability

### Greenwashing

In the absence of a standardized approach to ESG reporting, and the increasing demand for ESG practices, companies may resort to conveying of a false impression, or misleading information regarding how environmentally sound or beneficial their products or operations are. There is little accountability and transparency to hold them accountable to report accurate metrics when the very framework of the metrics can vary greatly across companies. Greenwashing is therefore a similar concept to *whitewashing*, which refers to providing misleading information to distract the public from a company's bad behavior. It exploits customers' and investors' authentic concerns for the environment and hinders their actual ability to make eco-friendly decisions when presented with misleading messages.

Greenwashing can take several forms, ranging from the use of colors and plants in advertising campaigns to evoke emotions related to eco-friendly activities, to outright false information such as claiming a product uses a specific numerical percentage of recycled content when in fact it does not. Companies can also advertise that a product is free from a given harmful substance, when in fact that harmful substance is banned for all products, and they are already required to do so. In another form of deception, companies may advertise the entirety of a product as eco-friendly when only one component of it is *green*, but the net effect is negative (e.g., *organic* cigarettes are still harmful to people's health). Finally, a company that creates its own certification to attest to its green practices without relying on a third party could be attempting to give only the impression of being green. The Federal Trade Commission in the United States has set guidelines on greenwashing as an attempt to protect customers against unlawful and unethical claims.

The ambiguities that exist today can make it easy for *greenwashing* performance in ways that inflate ESG impacts in reporting. This makes it difficult to set objective and effective strategies, while also diminishing the level of trust and reliability of ESG as a strategic opportunity. Greenwashing often takes the form of advertising claims with no reliable data to back them up or clear ESG commitment on the part of management. While greenwashing may be banned or illegal in certain jurisdictions, the various approaches and wide span of ESG issues make it difficult to rely on clear guidelines to define specific types of false ESG claims.

### Self-Reporting and Bias

Many ESG metrics are self-reported, which incentivizes companies to overstate their ESG impact and resort to overconfidence in their ability to benefit society and the environment. Because many industry-specific ESG standard setters can be either smaller entities or nonprofit organizations, there may not be an equivalent to an accounting standard for reporting that a company is obliged to adhere to. Many companies may not be aware of the strategic opportunities of ESG and view it as a burden, which would justify the effort to adhere to the least rigorous reporting practices. Without clear guidelines to adhere to realistic and measurable metrics that show accurate results, companies may overstate their performance with respect to ESG without an established framework to hold them accountable for their disclosures. Public companies are subject to accounting standards and they incorporate ESG metrics into them in different ways.

# The Perils of Disregarding Data

### Short-Term Profits Over Long-Term Strategy

Short-term profit seeking may be easier for companies to envision than incorporating ESG considerations, which may appear vague, complex, and irrelevant in their long-term approach when the future is filled with different variables. Short-term profitability may be the only sure guarantee a company can rely on for sustaining its operations, which would justify its unwillingness to take up the additional investment, resources, and time to developing an ESG strategy. Moreover, corporate cultures can be difficult to change, and management that does not appreciate the value of ESG on a strategic level may remain critical and minimize ESG practices to any requirements imposed on them. Finally, for public companies, investor pressure to demonstrate positive returns on a quarterly basis further incentivizes a short-term mindset that can simplify the level of strategic decision making or long-term view.

### Good Intentions, Bad Results

When ESG results are not well documented and monitored over time, funds may be mobilized for ESG purposes that in fact may bring negative overall consequences when the complexity of ESG issues is not properly taken into account. The lack of transparency and no knowledge of the impact of an ESG practice in this context could ultimately be harmful in several respects. This can be the case, particularly in philanthropy, which often makes use of no metrics and may focus solely on charitable giving without a full recognition of the strategic needs of the beneficiary. This outlook runs the risk of objectifying the recipients of donations and implying their inferiority as *needy* who can't help themselves, which may provide a short-term ego boost for the donor party but reinforce the cycle of dependence that is ultimately harmful to the recipient.

For instance, in post-earthquake Haiti, a massive shipment of clothing donations may disrupt the local emerging textile industry and hinder its growth, if not obliterate it completely. Haitian customers may find that donated clothing is of higher quality and lower cost than locally produced garments where the expertise and competitiveness are still being built but would be more beneficial for the country's economy in the long term. In Rwanda, after the genocide, a charitable institution may decide to donate eggs, disrupting the small poultry industry that would have otherwise created long-term jobs and secured the livelihoods of workers. Donations, moreover, can be unpredictable with changing objectives of the philanthropic institution and funds eventually running out. Thus, when the egg donations no longer arrive, the Rwandan community is left with no resources of its own to fulfill its needs.

Finally, lack of transparency to trace the use of donated funds can reinforce programs where a significant portion of donations are allocated to staff and operations without reaching the ultimate beneficiary that the program is meant to address.

### Blind Spots in ESG Programs

ESG can have several aspects in its implementation that may not be well integrated or documented in their entirety in the absence of a holistic framework. On the one hand, indicators may not be incorporated into the very design of an ESG endeavor or set a realistic baseline to compare over time, such that the view of results and monitoring and evaluation may be limited. On the other hand, different components of a company's operations may demonstrate different levels of adherence to ESG best practices, such that the net effect may ultimately be negative. On the other hand, a company may have limited visibility with regard to the ESG effects of some of its operations, such that it does not develop a comprehensive view of its impact and may enable unintended negative practices. For instance, a company that buys carbon credits to achieve a net-zero effect with respect to emissions may not be accounting for the heat it produces in its ocean infrastructure, which can be disrupting marine ecosystems. In a similar way, a company that prides itself for sustainable farming may not be accounting for the emissions produced in transporting food to markets. There may be little visibility across different components of the supply chain that are outsourced to suppliers or third parties.

# CHAPTER 5

# The Data Behind it All

In the early days, socially responsible, ethical, and values-based investing were considered to be something related to the activist movement in the 1960s and 1970s, and investors assumed that maximum returns would be sacrificed. Socially Responsible Investing (SRI) can be traced back to a number of ecclesiastical groups, including the Pioneer Fund that was launched in 1928 and the PAX World Fund, which used negative screening as selection criteria for investments. Customers have also been vocal in boycotting products offered by companies that have been seen as unethical or not socially responsible and have been effective in creating change for decades. In 1941, a consumer boycott was organized against Safeway, in Washington, DC, until they agreed to hire African Americans.

In the landscape of sustainability, socially responsible and environmental, social, and governance (ESG) data has evolved since the early days. Yet, there are over a dozen different ESG frameworks that offer industry-specific views. The reporting requirements are limited and only a subset of public companies offer reports that are published once a year.

## Sustainability Data Requires Context

There are many types of metrics and data that go into understanding sustainability, although the individual data components don't make sense until they are looked at through a specific lens, which is what the different frameworks and reporting standards offer. The individual data types are complex, varied, and unstructured, but in the context of a framework, the different elements contribute to the transparency and understanding of the intended audience. For example, a digitally native organization or a financial services company may not utilize any natural resources in the creation of their products and services. A financial services company could introduce a level of system risk, which is not relevant to most

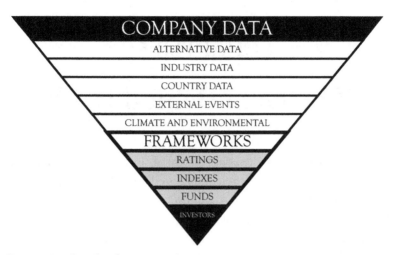

*Figure 5.1  Levels of company data*

© 2022 Cristina Dolan and Diana Barrero Zalles

digitally native software companies. The data that is utilized to measure sustainability across different industries is specific to each industry and the unique company characteristics within the industry context. A company like Netflix is in the entertainment space. Yet, it has a very different ESG profile compared to a company like Disney, which also has subsidiaries with very different industry profiles, such as has cruise lines and parks. The country in which business operations unfold represents another factor in the sustainability equation that needs to be considered. The data alone is meaningless without an appropriate lens and frameworks to analyze and represent the sustainability risk of organizations.

## Frameworks and Reporting Standards

There are a number of different methodologies and guidance frameworks that can be used for voluntary disclosure by an entity across a range of different industries and sectors. These frameworks and standards can differ significantly in how they cover and prioritize the role of stakeholders, investors, industry, and every level of detail. The evolution of reporting standards has grown over the past few decades from the initial Negative Screening and the early ESG overlays. There are numerous global reporting frameworks that each focus on different stakeholders and facets of sustainability. In September 2020, Global Reporting Initiative (GRI), CDP, CDSB, International Integrated Reporting Council (IIRC), and SASB put out a Statement of Intent to work together toward comprehensive corporate reporting.[1] In November 2020, the IIRC and the Sustainability Accounting Standards Board (SASB) announced their intention to merge and provide integrated and comprehensive corporate reporting standards.

## Selection Approaches for Sustainability Frameworks

### Negative Screening

Negative screening was used to eliminate the support of unethical companies. It can be traced back to centuries ago, when religious organizations wanted to focus on *responsible investing* and avoid unethical companies or *SIN* stocks.

### ESG Overlays

Investment overlays enable investors to integrate a variety of different lenses or personal convictions onto their investment approach, which could include aspects of ESG or impact investing.

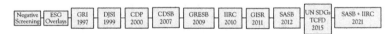

*Figure 5.2  The Beginning of Sustainability Frameworks*

© 2022 Cristina Dolan and Diana Barrero Zalles

### Global Reporting Initiative – GRI

The GRI guidelines[2] were the first Sustainability Reporting standards, published in 2000, three years after the organization was formed in Boston in response to the Exxon Valdez oil spill. Ceres, Tellus Institute,

---

[1]  https://29kjwb3armds2g3gi4lq2sx1-wpengine.netdna-ssl.com/wp-content/uploads/Statement-of-Intent-to-Work-Together-Towards-Comprehensive-Corporate-Reporting.pdf

[2]  www.globalreporting.org/about-gri/mission-history/

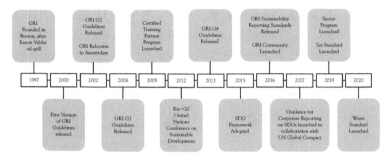

***Figure 5.3  Development of GRI events***

© 2022 Cristina Dolan & Diana Barrero Zalles

and the United Nations Environment Program (UNEP) initially formed the GRI, and in 2002, it moved its secretariat to Amsterdam, where it operates independently, yet continues to work closely with the UNEP and the United Nations Global Compact.

It is the first corporate social responsibility framework to be introduced, which is free to use, and is currently the most widely implemented. GRI is focused on measuring the impact that organizations have on the world and offers a multi-stakeholder process, which is different from other frameworks. For example, SASB is more aligned with sustainability information for investors.

The GRI framework has been updated several times, with ongoing updates each year. In 2017, they included guidance for corporate reporting on SDGs.[3]

## Dow Jones Sustainability Indices

As the first global index to track leading sustainability-driven public companies, it is considered a pioneer in sustainability investing and has raised the bar for corporate responsibility. Inclusion in the index, as a leading sustainability-driven company, is considered to be a badge of honor for companies, as it attracts more attention from financial analysts and long-term equity investors.[4]

---

[3]  Chart Copied from www.globalreporting.org/about-gri/mission-history/

[4]  https://onlinelibrary.wiley.com/doi/abs/10.1002/smj.3035

### Carbon Disclosure Project (CDP)

The standard for environmental disclosure is CDP, which was founded in 2000, to promote transparent and global disclosures reconciling the environmental and financial impact of operations. Countries, regions, or organizations are encouraged to disclose to their investors and customers by filling out the CDP questionnaires[5] that are focused on climate change, water security, and forests. Participating companies are provided with feedback on how they can improve their performance in these areas. Reports are sent to customers, investors, and pushed to the market for further reporting.

### Climate Disclosure Standards Board (CDSB)

The CDSB framework[6] is for reporting environmental and climate change information in mainstream corporate reports, annual reports, or the Form 10-K. It enables organizations to comply with the Financial Stability Board's Task Force on Climate-related Financial Disclosures (TCFD) recommendations by disclosing environmental and natural capital information. The CDSB was formed at the 2007 World Economic Forum annual meeting, and the CDP provides the secretariat. Utilizing the same principles as used in financial reporting, organizations can report on the environmental information in a standardized way.

### Global Real Estate Sustainability Benchmark (GRESB)

Founded in the Netherlands in 2009, GRESB is focused on the performance of global commercial real estate portfolios, real estate investment trusts (REITs), funds, asset managers, and developers utilizing ESG data, which includes governance and social factors. The GRESB utilizes a survey that is sent out in April, and the data provided is used to assess performance, management, and development to understand the quantitative and qualitative performance of operations.

---

[5] www.cdp.net/en/companies-discloser/how-to-disclose-as-a-company
[6] www.cdsb.net/what-we-do/reporting-frameworks

### International Integrated Reporting Council (IIRC)

The IIRC is a coalition that includes a variety of different entities from policy makers, academia, regulators, exchanges, providers of financial capital, accountants, businesses, and other broad global communities for the adoption of Integrated Reporting and value creation, to improve sustainability and financial stability. In 2020, the IIRC announced its plans to merge with the SASB in 2021.

### Global Initiative for Sustainability Ratings (GISR)

The goal of GISR is to direct the financial, human, social, and natural capital of organizations toward sustainable development. It is a ratings framework that measures excellence in sustainability performance by utilizing ESG data to produce ratings. The GISR framework is made up of principles, performance, weights applied to indicators, and quality corporate strategy, management, and culture relative to sustainability. The Ratings Hub provides sustainability ratings, ranking, and indexes that can be used by investors, companies, governments, and academics for investment, strategy, and policy.

### Sustainability Accounting Standards Board (SASB)

Although the SASB is younger than the other frameworks, it is gaining momentum with its industry- and sector-specific material sustainability standards for disclosure. Organizations like Blackrock have announced their support of the SASB, further promoting its adoption across industries. When compared with the more popular reporting framework, GRI, SASB is better aligned with representing how the world impacts a company through an investment community lens and is used by U.S. public companies. The SASB materiality framework enables investors to understand the financial impacts of sustainability on a business, which align with shareholder and investor risk. The SASB R-Factor (the R represents responsibility) is a proprietary ESG scoring system that leverages the SASB Materiality Map for greater transparency and insights into financially material risks. It has announced a merger with IIRC will be completed in 2021.

*Task Force on Climate-Related Financial Disclosures (TCFD)*

The TCFD was established by the Financial Stability Board in December of 2015, with the goal of establishing voluntary climate-related financial risk disclosure guidelines for companies to communicate to stakeholders and investors. The core elements of these disclosures are structured around governance, strategy, risk management, metrics, and targets. The consistent reporting will enable markets to manage climate-related risks. It is led by a taskforce of 31 members from G20 countries and has been chaired by Michael Bloomberg.[7]

## ESG Data Components

Today, the basic ESG components fall into three basic categories, and each category has a number of subcategories that vary by industry. For example, water as a natural resource is critical to beverage companies and not as relevant for the technology sector. Multiple companies in the same industry may have a completely different carbon footprint. Digitally native firms will represent a different set of environmental issues or work conditions. The data sources could vary by industry or framework.

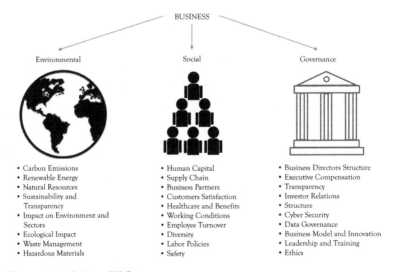

| Environmental | Social | Governance |
| --- | --- | --- |
| • Carbon Emissions | • Human Capital | • Business Directors Structure |
| • Renewable Energy | • Supply Chain | • Executive Compensation |
| • Natural Resources | • Business Partners | • Transparency |
| • Sustainability and Transparency | • Customers Satisfaction | • Investor Relations |
| • Impact on Environment and Sectors | • Healthcare and Benefits | • Structure |
| • Ecological Impact | • Working Conditions | • Cyber Security |
| • Waste Management | • Employee Turnover | • Data Governance |
| • Hazardous Materials | • Diversity | • Business Model and Innovation |
|  | • Labor Policies | • Leadership and Training |
|  | • Safety | • Ethics |

*Figure 5.4 Major ESG issues*
© 2022 Cristina Dolan & Diana Barrero Zalles

---

[7] www.fsb-tcfd.org/about/#

Employee turnover isn't always reported but could be extracted from external sources or scraped off the web. Sponsorships of social programs may be announced in press releases or communicated through social feeds.

### Data Suppliers

In addition to the variety of frameworks, there are a variety of different data companies. Some data companies offer narrow data feeds captured from sources, which include social media sentiment, news analysis, satellite images, data breaches, regulatory fines, employee turnover, and board composition metrics, with a level of analysis that is relevant to specific industries, geographies, and companies. They will clean, normalize, and analyze the data within a context specific to client needs as a feed or within a dashboard. These companies may need to employ multiple different processes to gather data from different sources with a level of human research to fill in the data gaps. The data sources, processes, and methodologies will vary based on the firm, and the goals and will generate different types of financial metrics.

Some ESG data companies construct ratings specific to companies, countries, and industries that are aggregated from a variety of different sources. While the yearly sustainability reports that are published by public companies offer some insights, they can be biased and may not represent a holistic understanding. Rating agencies and investors will collect hundreds of data points to analyze hundreds of different sustainability- and ESG-related metrics. Some may utilize proprietary or niche data that

**Figure 5.5  ESG data processing**

© 2022 Cristina Dolan and Diana Barrero Zalles

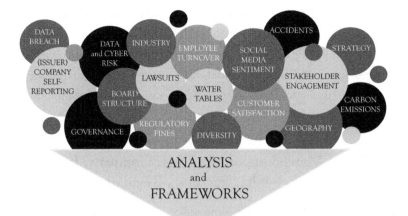

*Figure 5.6 Sources of ESG data to be analyzed*

© 2022 Cristina Dolan and Diana Barrero Zalles

may be relevant to a specific industry, generating hundreds of insights from the analysis of the data. For example, understanding changes in water supply may be critical to sustainability and growth of beverage companies located in specific geographies. Most of the data is unstructured and requires context and integration into the appropriate sustainability frameworks to extract valuable insights. Machine learning and artificial intelligence solutions are evolving to create more sophisticated insights and predictions on risk factors.

### Country-Level Sustainability Data

One important factor in corporate sustainability and potential material financial risks is inherently linked to the geography in which the entity and its customers unfold their activities. There are a number of country sustainability rankings that offer insights on material financial impact on the risks associated with governments or the effect of climate change in a specific region or geography. In 2019, the World Bank launched a free and open Sovereign ESG Data Portal[8] that offers sovereign-level ESG data. The platform should enable improved transparency across 67

---

[8] www.worldbank.org/en/news/press-release/2019/10/29/world-bank-launches-sovereign-esg-data-portal

indicators and the 17 Sustainable Development Goals for all World Bank countries, enabling transparency for private investment in emerging markets and developing countries. Government policies are tightly correlated with the sustainability of companies, the economy, and the environment. Increasing visibility at every level makes it easier for all stakeholders to contribute to positive change.

## Different Viewpoints on the Data: Company, Investor, Stakeholder, Partners, Regulators

Depending on how the data is being utilized, the representation will look different. Some argue that the corporate reporting process is limited in detail, time span, and frequency. In addition, self-reporting can often be *biased*, which is why some funds do not rely on self-reported ESG data. The understanding of ESG risk needs context, which includes industry and country information with added layers of analysis and alternative data sources.

Sustainability data lacks standardization, and reporting looks back in time, rather than being forward-looking. Sometimes, companies do provide data on current events, but it is rare to find data that looks into the future. One analysis may look at the outcomes, which may include the number of incidents, breaches, or fines that have been incurred by a given company, while another will look at the governance structure that has been implemented to reduce risk in the future. There generally is no standard representation of timeframe or use of outcomes, as opposed to the existing governance structures that companies have put in place to

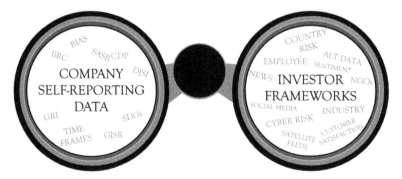

*Figure 5.7 Various lenses for ESG data*

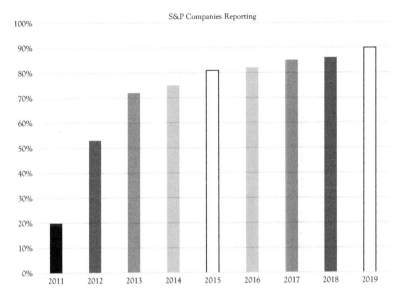

**Figure 5.8** *Governance and Accounting Institute analysis or reporting by GICS classification*

© 2022 Cristina Dolan and Diana Barrero Zalles

reduce risk. In addition, every industry will have a different set of data points. Companies within an industry can also differ substantially, for example, Disney and Netflix. Disney has a larger carbon footprint than Netflix, which is primarily a digital company.

### Company Reporting

Companies typically report once a year. The number of S&P companies that provided some type of sustainability report in 2019 has grown to 90 percent, which represents 80 percent of the outstanding equity of the largest U.S. companies, according to the Governance and Accountability Institute.[9] In just nine years, this percentage has increased from just 20 percent in 2011 to 90 percent in 2019.

---

[9] Global Newswire: 90% of S&P 500 Index Companies Publish Sustainability Reports in 2019, G&A Announces in its Latest Annual 2020 Flash Report, July 16, 2020. www.globenewswire.com/news-release/2020/07/16/2063434/0/

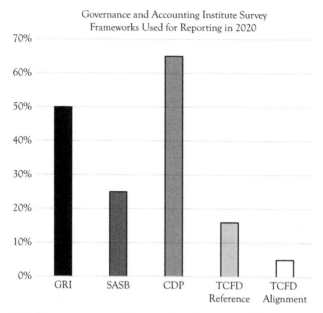

Figure 5.9 *Governance and Accounting Institute, Inc 2020 research reporting survey*

© 2022 Cristina Dolan and Diana Barrero Zalles

While the number of companies disclosing these metrics has increased, the frameworks that are utilized for this reporting have varied. A 2020 G&A Institutes Survey shows the greatest number of participants utilized the GRI, which was initially released with the GRI framework in early 2000.

While there could be some sustainability-related news or events that are shared in quarterly reports throughout the year, most companies do not provide additional information or report on this matter throughout the year. The completeness within the different formats utilized can also vary, making it difficult to compare the raw results across an industry. Reports tend to look back in time. It is rare to find companies that offer insights into the future, and if there is a data point reflecting future sustainability risks, it is typically presented in a non-standard time format. Most companies will not offer insights about risks into the future because this may also provide insights on vulnerabilities to competitors and could create liabilities.

en/90-of-S-P-500-Index-Companies-Publish-Sustainability-Reports-in-2019-G-A-Announces-in-its-Latest-Annual-2020-Flash-Report.html

# Company Strategy

One component of corporate sustainability involves the creation of an ESG strategy that engages all stakeholders within a company, from the board and senior executives, down to each employee within the organization. Compensation needs to be tied to the KPIs and measured results, especially at the board and management levels. If the strategy isn't established, measured, communicated, and rewarded, these goals will not be realized.

## Company Bias in Reporting

Today, company reporting is not standardized or complete, even within standardized frameworks, forcing analysts to utilize a combination of proprietary data points and models to calculate a company's ESG and sustainability ratings in order to avoid bias. It can be an extremely time-consuming process to gather these data points across every ESG-related metric, especially if the discrete data points are acquired from a variety of different providers in different formats.

## Regulatory Disclosure Requirements

Sustainability disclosure regulations and benchmarking initiatives in the UK and European Union (EU) provide a lens for shareholders to measure corporate performance based on sustainability and climate-change risks. The EU disclosure regulations came into force in December 2019, and into effect for financial market participants and financial advisors after March 10, 2021, in order to enable informed ESG-related investment decisions. The EU Taxonomy on Sustainable Finance provides guidelines for large organizations and multinational enterprises, and it is considered one of the most important developments for sustainable finance. The guidelines for disclosure differ by size and require companies that offer financial products to provide sustainability insights for each product with visibility on the approach and composition. The UK's Financial Conduct Authority (FCA) is also requiring all companies with premium listings to provide annual sustainability and climate-related disclosures, separate from annual financial disclosures. This FCA required annual sustainability report must be compliant with the TCFD.

| | GRI | SASB | IIRC | UN SDGs | CDSB | TCFD | GRESB |
|---|---|---|---|---|---|---|---|
| Subject | Sustainability | Sustainability | Non-Financial and Financial | Non-Financial | Climate Change | Climate Change | Sustainability |
| Structure | Standards | Standards | Framework | Principles | Framework | Framework | Framework |
| Scope | General | Industry-specific | General | General | General | General and sector-specific | Real Estate |
| Audience | All stakeholders | Investors | Investors | All stakeholders | Investors | Investors, lenders and insurance underwriters | Investors, fund managers, commercial real estate portfolios, REITS and developers |

**Figure 5.10 Different approaches to sustainability reporting**

© 2022 Cristina Dolan and Diana Barrero Zalles

As momentum toward ESG Reporting increases, so has the trend toward simplifying these reporting metrics. The World Economic Forum and the International Business Council, together with Deloitte, EY, KPMG, and PwC, have released a White Paper on *Measuring Stakeholder Capitalism: Towards Common Metrics and Consistent Report of Sustainable Value Creation.*[10] The four pillars of these core metrics and disclosures center around the principles of governance, planet, people, and prosperity. The recommended metrics were created with the goals of maintaining consistency with existing standards and frameworks and general applicability.

## Investor Lenses Differ

The investor view of entities can vary significantly based on the investment thesis. For example, some investors want to avoid investing in specific industries, risky countries, or immoral companies and will utilize a negative screening approach. Early investors didn't have data or tools for a metrics-driven approach, yet they were able to use negative screening to avoid unwanted industries or companies. Some investors utilize a hybrid approach of integrating ESG philosophy into their portfolio. Values-based investing is different from value investing, although companies that adhere to sustainability investment tend to generate greater returns and tend to be more flexible and adaptable when confronted with unexpected circumstances like the COVID-19 crisis. Impact investing

---

[10] www3.weforum.org/docs/WEF_IBC_Measuring_Stakeholder_Capitalism_Report_2020.pdf

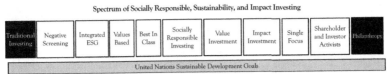

*Figure 5.11 Investment strategies for sustainability*

© 2022 Cristina Dolan and Diana Barrero Zalles

is a philosophy that a number of family offices and private equity firms attempt to adopt, but the impact is often difficult to measure, especially with publicly held companies. While some investors only want to invest in industries, entities, countries, or portfolios that are focused on sustainability, it is easier to make changes as a shareholder or investor activist.

## ESG Factors are Risk Factors

Today, ESG ratings are used to understand organizational risk from a different perspective, which includes how prepared an organization is for the future. ESG factors are metrics of risk, which quants and investors are interested in understanding. Unfortunately, there isn't any significant consistency in the data. Quality in reporting, especially with respect to financial impact or SDG materiality, isn't available.

In addition, investors take different approaches on the use of sustainability or ESG data for investment decisions. The utilization of the available data is applied to a variety of different investment strategies that may be as simple as negative screening or a more analytical approach to generate positive returns while achieving environmental or social KPIs for the portfolio, for example, the reduction of carbon emissions metrics across the portfolio. Each of the strategies utilizes different types of data to achieve their investing goals.

## UN Sustainable Development Goals

Alignment with the United Nations Sustainable Development Goals is one approach for responsible investing to participate in shaping real-world outcomes for the most pressing challenges faced by humans globally. The SDGs provide a high-level framework that investors can use as a preliminary guideline.

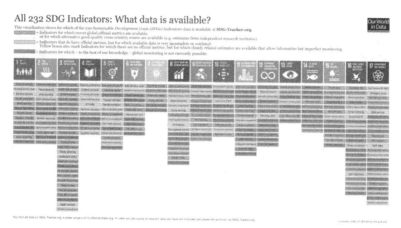

*Figure 5.12 SDG indicators for investment*[11]

## Negative Screening

Before the development of data sets for socially responsible investing, early investors avoided doing business or investing in companies that were not ethical or aligned with specific values. This approach is called negative screening, and is still in use today. The data that is used is based on the criteria set by the values. For example, an investor may want to avoid unethical companies or *sin stocks*, which would include companies involved in areas like weapons, tobacco, adult entertainment, child labor, entertainment, alcohol, or gambling. The data requirements for the implementation of a negative screening strategy are less sophisticated compared to other strategies.

## Values Based

Investors who invest based on their values will choose companies that are aligned with their personal values, which may include the environment, community, diversity, or other criteria. ESG ratings provide insights on how companies align with specific values and are socially beneficial.

---

[11] Open-source data from Our World in Data: https://ourworldindata.org/sdg-tracker-update

## Best in Class

One approach that has been heavily scrutinized is best in class, because it allows for investments in companies in sectors that may be considered controversial. For example, an oil company that is managed better than its competitors could be included in a fund. Leading technology firms have been included in many ESG funds, which has been considered controversial if the data governance or employee diversity is considered to be an issue of concern.

## Value Investment

Some investors are focused on creating value, and ESG metrics provide insights on how well a company is managed and have the ability to provide an additional level of transparency for value investors. Companies can achieve good ESG ratings through proper governance, even if the company is in a business that isn't considered beneficial for the environment. Companies that are producing clean energy or products that are good for the environment can receive poor ESG ratings or scores if they do not have the proper governance or if they do not treat their employees well. It is clear that companies that are well managed tend to be more resilient, and ESG scores are an additional datapoint to understand how organizations are run.

## Impact Investment

The hardest investment strategy to prove is the value of the impact that an investment can make, especially if it is within a publicly held company. The direct correlation between the outcomes from an investment is hard to extract within complex business models. Private equity funds have greater insights on the companies they invest in and are in a better position to measure the impact of their investments.

## Single Focus

There are a number of investors and funds that focus on a special theme, for example, diversity or clean energy.

*Shareholder Activist*

Investors who avoid companies that are not producing outcomes aligned with ESG goals lose out on the opportunity to voice their opinions as shareholders. Shareholder activists can vote to create change within an organization to achieve specific outcomes.

## Investment Growth in ESG Sustainable Funds

The investment levels in sustainable companies hit an all-time high in the year 2020, which demonstrates why there is a need to understand how investors are defining sustainable, responsible, or ESG investing.

The following chart shows the growth of investment into funds that are considered ESG integration, impact, and sustainable U.S. funds.[12] The assets under management of these funds has surpassed $1 trillion in 2020 according to Morningstar. During the COVID-19 crisis, Morningstar reported performance in sustainable equity funds fared better than conventional market indexes.[13]

The Callan Institute July 2020 USA ESG investor survey[14] published results indicate that 42 percent of institutional investors, 57 percent of foundations, 63 percent of endowments, and 47 percent of funds with over $20 billion under management incorporated some ESG factors into their investment decisions. Furthermore, 56 percent of the survey respondents did not incorporate ESG strategies into investment decision making because of the lack of clarity on the benefits of doing so.

In 2020, the OECD reported[15] that one-fifth of professionally managed U.S. assets have engaged in some form of sustainable investing, yet there is some concern by investors that ESG products are not clearly labeled with transparent methodologies. The U.S. SIF Foundation's 2020

---

[12] www.morningstar.com/articles/1019195/a-broken-record-flows-for-us-sustainable-funds-again-reach-new-heights

[13] www.morningstar.com/articles/970108/us-sustainable-funds-weathering-coronavirus-correction-better-than-most-funds

[14] www.callan.com/wp-content/uploads/2020/09/Callan-2020-ESG-Survey.pdf

[15] www.oecd.org/daf/Sustainable-and-Resilient-Finance.pdf

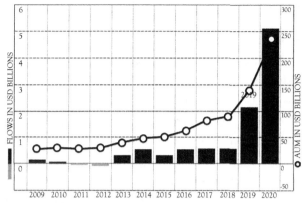

*Figure 5.13  Flows on U.S. sustainable funds*

© 2022 Cristina Dolan and Diana Barrero Zalles

biennial *Report on US Sustainable and Impact Investing Treads*[16] released in November 2020, found that sustainable investing assets account for one in three dollars under professional management, which at the time of the report accounted for $17.2 trillion in the United States.

### Future Alignment of Frameworks and Reporting

In September 2020, the five leading global organizations for frameworks and standard setting issued a joint press release[17] announcing a move to work together with a shared vision to enable a more comprehensive corporate reporting. They also agreed to work closely with leading organizations, which include the World Economic International Business Council, the European Commission, and the IOSCO. This is a critical step to enabling transparency and the connection between sustainability and the material financial impact of ESG.

---

[16] www.ussif.org/blog_home.asp?Display=155

[17] www.sasb.org/wp-content/uploads/2020/09/Press-release-Comprehensive-Corporate-Reporting-paper-11-Sep-20.pdf

## Governance

The variations in reporting standards, frameworks, metrics, and terms have created some concerns, especially for investors and global regulators. ESG and sustainability are broad, and they encompass many different data points. The U.S. Commissioner of the SEC, Elad L. Roisman, gave a speech[18] on July 7, 2020, where he discussed the scope of SEC jurisdiction and the requirement for public companies to discuss the financial materiality of ESG-related risks, yet expressed a concern with *greenwashing* by some asset managers and has begun to scrutinize claims. The lack of transparency and standards for the use of ESG, green, and sustainable make it difficult for retail investors to understand or compare the results. A taxonomy report[19] for screening environmentally sustainable activities has been published by The European Commission's Technical Expert Group on Sustainable Finance. The report contains recommendations on how companies and financial institutions can make disclosures using the taxonomy.

---

[18] www.sec.gov/news/speech/roisman-keynote-society-corporate-governance-national-conference-2020

[19] https://knowledge4policy.ec.europa.eu/publication/sustainable-finance-teg-final-report-eu-taxonomy_en

# CHAPTER 6

# Case Studies of Data Companies That Have Developed Solutions

## Financial Data

As global brands and companies like Apple, Microsoft, Amazon, Alphabet, and Alibaba grow in influence and market capitalization, even at levels that eclipse the gross domestic product of most countries, except for the top 16, it is clear there is a need for companies to engage in managing sustainability responsibly. The influence of these companies can be extensive and involve many stakeholders engaged as employees, employee families, neighborhoods, suppliers, customers, vendors, investors, or other roles of community members.

As companies engage in sustainability goal setting, self-reporting, and self-governance, they create value and reduce risk. There is a part of a company's community that defines the value of an organization based on how it manages sustainability. The investment community, which includes customers, will establish a price based on the perception of sustainability risk and value generation. There is a part of a company's community of stakeholders that build the products and provide the services. They choose to work with the company or engage with the company based on their perceptions of its ethics and value generation.

Companies that don't manage sustainability create financial risk for investors, as well as employment risk for employees. When a company closes up its operations or goes out of business because customers and investors no longer value the organization, its products, or its services, the community will suffer from the lost value creation. The local town may

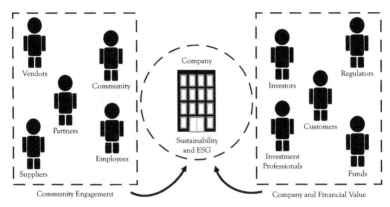

**Figure 6.1  The value of an organization is established by the community of stakeholders**

© 2022 Cristina Dolan and Diana Barrero Zalles

lose tax revenue, which will impact the schools and other government services. The suppliers, partners, and vendors will also suffer a financial impact if they lose business. This is why, having mechanisms by which companies can be rated becomes valuable for all of the stakeholders. There are many different approaches that are used by the investment community, which go beyond corporate reporting frameworks. Some investors don't even use corporate self-reported sustainability data, as they want to avoid any type of bias. This is why, there is value in the analysis done by rating agencies and indexes to evaluate companies based on industry.

The perceived ESG rating of an organization has two major effects. The first is the level of commitment from the community, which drives

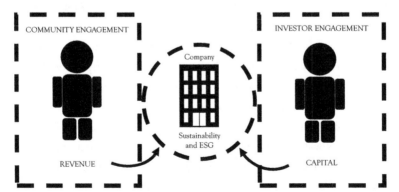

**Figure 6.2  Sources of revenue and capital for ESG endeavors**

© 2022 Cristina Dolan and Diana Barrero Zalles

opportunities for revenue generation, and the second is the perception of investors on the level of risk, which impacts access to capital for growth. Both of the forces play a major role in the success of an organization, which is why it is important to have metrics to measure sustainability from a variety of different lenses.

Credit rating agencies play a major role in assessing the credit risk of companies, countries, and financial products, by issuing a rating score. Moody's, Standard & Poor's, and Fitch are the major credit rating agencies, which have focused on an entity's financial ability to repay different types of loans, bonds, or debt for over a century. The assessments of these rating services directly affect an organization's access to capital.

## Where Ratings Fit Into the Financial Ecosystem

It is important to understand the role of sustainability ratings in the overall ESG financial ecosystem as defined by the OECD Business and Finance Outlook 2020 Report.[1] Rating providers are part of the financial intermediation chain between the issues of a security, stock, bond, sovereign bonds, or other financial instrument and the end investors who take the risk and earn the rewards.

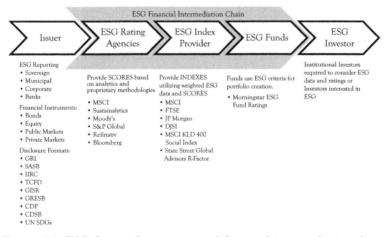

*Figure 6.3  ESG financial ecosystem and financial intermediation chain*
© 2022 Cristina Dolan and Diana Barrero Zalles

---

[1] www.oecd.org/daf/Sustainable-and-Resilient-Finance.pdf

The ESG rating providers generate assessments of financial instruments from ESG financial issuers that may be offered on public markets or through private channels. Disclosures by the financial issuers may make up one of the data points, although the ratings providers analyze additional information to offer metrics and scores that enable comparisons across industries, countries, or other market segments. The sources and other quantitative data used to calculate the scores are communicated to investors in the context of the defined framework and rating or scoring mechanism. These ratings provide a benchmark for performance, which can be incorporated in the communications that asset managers and institutional investors provide for end investors.

## Sustainability Ratings and Indexes

Sustainability ratings offer a different type of metric for understanding the materiality of financial risk of an organization. It offers predictions on how well a company is managed, sustainability efforts, and an indication of the level of agility that will enable the entity to adapt to external forces like climate change or a global pandemic. As the intangible value of organizations increases, the financial material impact to a brand or other intangible assets is critical to the sustainability of an organization. A report by AON and the Ponemon Institute in 2019 indicated that the intangible value of the S&P 500 had reached 83 percent, and only 40 years ago, it was only 13 percent.[2] The ESG ratings offer the ability to use other metrics to measure intangible risks that could affect the sustainability or agility of an organization.

Many investors utilize the ESG ratings as criteria for credit or investments. As sustainability investing has grown in popularity and volume, signals have become more widely used as a metric of risk. In addition, to find the material investment, signals can be a strategy to achieve alpha and positive portfolio performance. An Institutional Investor article, *Where ESG Fails*,[3] from October 09 in 2019, debates the performance of sustainable companies because Fortune 500 companies between

---

[2] www.aon.com/thought-leadership/ponemoninstitutereport.jsp

[3] www.institutionalinvestor.com/article/b1hm5ghqtxj9s7/Where-ESG-Fails

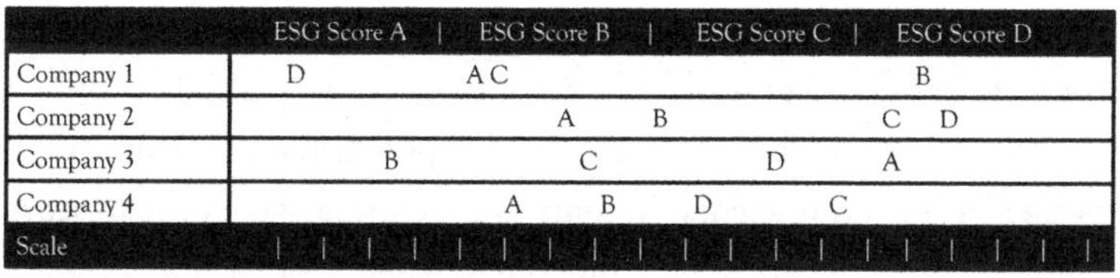

| | ESG Score A | ESG Score B | ESG Score C | ESG Score D |
|---|---|---|---|---|
| Company 1 | D | A C | | B |
| Company 2 | | A | B | C D |
| Company 3 | B | C | D | A |
| Company 4 | | A B | D | C |
| Scale | | | | |

**Figure 6.4  Variability in ESG ratings**

© 2022 Cristina Dolan & Diana Barrero Zalles

2015 and 2017 outperformed the MSCI World Stock Index by 3.9 percent. Today, the reporting standards have improved in addition to the correlation between metrics and financial materiality by industry. Unfortunately, the rating agencies are not yet as aligned on ESG ratings as they are on issuer credit ratings. The following is a sample of some securities that were ranked by a variety of ESG rating organizations in 2019, taken from the OECD Business and Finance Outlook Report. It is clear that the ESG ratings from the top three providers have very little overlap.

When comparing the ESG ratings for an entity, the ESG ratings have a wider range of values than the issuer credit rating for each entity. Credit ratings are regulated and measure an organization's ability to pay back debt. While sustainability is an indicator of credit risk, ESG ratings are not regulated. It is argued that ESG should be incorporated into credit rating scores as it is an indication or the organization's sustainability into the future.

Each of the different ratings organizations has their own proprietary methodologies and data points, with different metrics and weightings. This is why, the end results across frameworks are different. The data sources and composition of the hundreds of different data points may vary. This leads to a divergence in metrics between rating agencies. A paper published in August 2019 by a team of MIT researchers, *Aggregate Confusion: The Divergence of ESG Ratings*,[4] explored the differences in the scope, measurements, and weights of the categories and concluded that scope and measurement differences play a significant role in the divergence of the scoring. The researchers observed top ESG Rating agencies,

---

[4] https://papers.ssrn.com/sol3/papers.cfm?abstract_id=3438533

which include MSCI, Sustainalytics, S&P Global, Moody's, and Refinitiv, analyzing each of their proprietary methodologies. The general taxonomy of 65 data categories was similar, yet the data points and the scope of the data differ by the rating agency. In some cases, a rating agency might score the number of past incidences or outcomes, while another may evaluate the entity's current practices to calculate part of the score. The source of the data may also derive from a company's sustainability disclosure, which may be subject to bias due to self-reporting. Still, other agencies may choose to source specific data points from independent third parties. It is this variation in the ratings that challenges the implementation of ESG investor strategies. There is an inability to utilize uniform ESG disclosure formats and ratings of specific companies to achieve optimal portfolio performance. While credit ratings are indicative of an entity's ability to repay debt, there isn't a widespread level of confidence with regard to the ESG score correlation to performance. Thus, it is very difficult to utilize the existing data to explain ESG as a performance differentiator for an investment strategy, whether on the upside or the downside, in the short or long term.

The marginal benefit of having access to third-party rating agencies, and not having to rely on company disclosures, offers the ability to avoid reporting bias in the disclosures. Many investment firms utilize a combination of different ratings and reports in creating their investment thesis. The rating agencies utilize the same business model for sustainability and ESG ratings as they do for traditional credit ratings. The investors pay for the reports, and the companies do not pay or have an influence in the results reported in these sustainability and ESG reports and scores.

There has been criticism regarding ESG rating agencies, as well as the use of proprietary assessment methodologies with limited transparency. The correlation between the different ratings is limited, and the differences in the scoring limit companies' motivation to adjust or improve their practices in order to achieve better scores. The goal of the scoring should go beyond the analysis of material financial risk due to ESG; it should enable companies to make changes to improve scores, which could impact the valuations set by the investment community. Different stakeholders require a different lens, although most of the rating agencies are aligned with the lens of financial investment. In addition, the evolution of reporting frameworks and regulations have provided additional metrics and lenses for ESG reporting, adding to the various dimensions already in existence across industries. This poses yet another set of different characteristics relative to sustainability to report on.

As sustainability has become more popular, the use of ratings, analysis, and indexes have become more widespread as well, especially since the European Parliament and EU member states have agreed on new sustainability disclosure rules. Unfortunately, the lack of standardization, proprietary methodologies, differences in data sources, variability in parameter weights, and a lack of transparency create a significant level of inconsistency across rating approaches. This in turn creates confusion for investors and issuing companies. There has been a high level of consolidation in ESG rating and analysis companies after 2008, and credit rating firms are expanding their coverage of sustainability metrics and product offerings as investor interest continues to grow.

## The Growth and Consolidation of the Leading Sustainability Ratings Companies

### Vigeo Eiris and Moody's

The first rating agency for sustainability was Eiris, which was owned by the Eiris Foundation and launched in 1983 in France. Vigeo was created by Nicole Notat in 2002 and acquired by the French rating agency Arèse. In 2015, Vigeo and Eiris announced their merger, and the organization was renamed Vigeo Eiris. In 2019, the firm was acquired by Moody's. The organization is focused on sustainable value creation and economic performance through responsible investment. Moody's has acquired a number of companies in the ESG space, including Four Twenty Seven, which focuses on physical climate risks.

### Kinder, Lydenberg & Domini (KLD) and MSCI

The U.S. rating agency, Kinder, Lydenberg & Domini (KLD) was established in 1989, by Peter Kinder, Steve Lydenberg, and Amy Domini. In 1990, KLD's co-founder Amy Domini launched the Domini 400 Social Index (MSCI KLD 400 Social Index), which was one of the first social indexes created to provide a tool for socially conscious investors. KLD was later acquired by Risk Metrics in 2009. A year later, in 2010, MSCI acquired Risk Metrics, and the database product was renamed to MSCI KLD to differentiate it from the MSCI dataset. The index was renamed MSCI KLD 400 Social Index in 2010.

## MSCI

MSCI has expanded through a number of acquisitions, and eventually expanded into the ESG space. The Capital Group, founded in Los Angeles in 1964, developed the Capital International World indexes, which were acquired by Morgan Stanley in 1998. The indexes were renamed the Morgan Stanley Capital International Indexes (MSCI Indexes). MSCI expanded into the ESG research data and rating space through continued acquisitions, including RiskMetrics Group in 2010, which had previously acquired Institutional Shareholder Services (ISS) in 2007. Other acquisitions include Innovest Strategic Value Advisors in 2009 and KLD Research and Analytics in 2009. MSCI ESG Research is the result of combining Innovest Strategic Value Advisors and KLD Research and Analytics and is the basis for the MSCI ESG Indexes. MeasureRisk, a provider of risk assessment tools for hedge fund investors, was acquired in 2010.

### Sustainalytics and Morningstar

In 1992, Michael Jantzi launched Jantzi Research to evaluate the sustainability performance of companies. Later in 2009, after a merger with Sustainalytics, the company was later renamed Sustainalytics. Through partnerships and joint ventures, the company launched Scoris, Jantzi Social Index, SiRi Group, Dutch Sustainability Research, Global Ethical Standard, Glass Lewis corporate governance raw data, and the FTSE Russell ESG Indexes. In 2017, Morningstar acquired 40 percent of Sustainalytics, and later acquired the remaining 70 percent in 2020. In addition to company sustainability ratings, Sustainalytics offers products including Country ESG Risk Research & Ratings, Carbon Risk Ratings, Sustainable Products Research and Human Rights Radar. Sustainalytics has acquired a number of firms, including ESG Analytics, Responsible Research, and Share Dimension. Sustainalytics has grown to become a leader in sustainability, ESG risk ratings, and corporate governance metrics. In 2018, Yahoo Finance added Sustainalytics scores to the platform. In addition, Morningstar offers sustainability ratings for funds in addition to sustainability research, data, and analytics.

## S&P Global, RobecoSAM, DJSI, and Trucost

Retro Ringger founded SAM in 1995, an investment company focused on sustainability based in Zurich, Switzerland. In 1999, SAM and Dow Jones launched the Dow Jones Sustainability Indexes (DJSI), which were the first of their kind. SAM developed the methodology for the DJSI Corporate Sustainability Assessment for 60 industries. In 2006, SAM was acquired by Robeco, and in 2013, the company was rebranded RobecoSam. In 2006, SAM founded a division that provides company benchmarking reports with strengths and weaknesses mapped against best in class and sustainability metrics. In 2019, S&P Global acquired the ESG ratings business from RobecoSAM, to build on the existing relationships and offer more transparent and comprehensive ESG solutions for customers by utilizing the RobecoSAM unique datasets and methodology. In 2006, S&P acquired Trucost, which was founded in 2000. It is part of S&P global and is a market intelligence company focused on carbon data, environmental data, and risk analysis associated with climate change, natural resource constraint, and broader environmental, social, and government factors.

## Refinitiv ESG

Refinitiv ESG scores (formerly Thomson Reuters Corporate Responsibility Ratings, TRCRR) go back to the year 2002. In 2009, Refinitiv acquired ASSET4, a business founded in 2003 that focused on developing, constructing, and maintaining ratings. It pulled over 250 key performance indicators and over 750 individual data points it provided data across a variety of different pillars. The data points have different ratings, or can be assigned a different Relative Level of Importance (RLI), depending on the pillars and industry under consideration. They offer a variety of metrics from best-in-class data to industry comparisons in order to meet investors' specific needs and investment criteria.

### Bloomberg

In 2020, Bloomberg announced the launch of proprietary ESG scores utilizing a proprietary quant model that utilizes industry frameworks, research, and analysis to close data gaps and eliminate bias. Bloomberg offers an SASB ESG Index, which utilizes the State Street Global Advisors R-Factor proprietary ESG scoring system based on the SASB standards. In addition, Bloomberg offers third-party ESG scores through its Bloomberg terminal.

### ISS (Institutional Shareholder Services)

In 1985, ISS was founded to provide analytics, eventually growing to become a leader in corporate governance. Ethix SRI Advisors was acquired by ISS in 2015 to expand into Europe. In 2018, ISS acquired the German ESG rating company oekom research AG. Eventually Deutsche Borse acquired a majority share of ISS in 2020.

## Growth of AI Solutions

There are a number of young small companies focused on specific narrow areas of sustainability data and analytics, and the consolidation of providers will continue as ESG popularity increases. In addition, there are several different investor approaches toward sustainable investing, which arise from various different needs from the investors themselves. For example, Arabesque uses artificial intelligence and non-financial ESG data successfully to build new quant models for sustainability. The ability to use AI to extract better insights, statistics, and comparisons from a variety of different data sources is used by investors to gain a better understanding of the many dimensions of risk. Arabesque S-Ray is a quantitative data tool that can be used to measure the performance of the world's largest listed companies. Another example is Sensefolio, which utilizes artificial intelligence and natural language processing to extract company ethical performance by analyzing unstructured social feeds, news, and financial reports. Akadia is a company based in India that offers granular insights on ESG performance for companies of all sizes.

## Evolving ESG, Sustainable and Responsible Investing Standards

The ESG data space is relatively young and is evolving at the same time as the standards, regulations, and investment philosophies are all developing. At each point along the ESG financial intermediation chain, there are many differences that make it challenging to compare the metrics from one organization to another in the value chain. While there have been commitments toward better alignment by the organizations that represent the issuer reporting frameworks, this poses significant challenges because there are many differences across the board that create confusion. The spectrum of investment philosophies requires different datasets and approaches. For example, a fund that is focused on companies with female executives will require a narrow dataset to meet its investment goals. Decreasing the level of carbon emissions across a portfolio or fund over a period of time, on the other hand, requires a completely different set of data points.

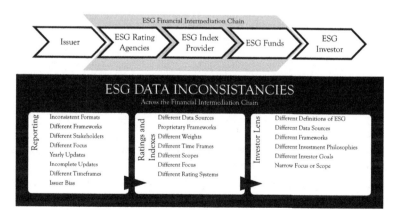

*Figure 6.5  ESG financial intermediation chain and data inconsistencies*

Sustainability, responsible investing and ESG have different meanings to different investors. There is a need for better consistency and alignment across the value chain, which is aligned with all the reporting frameworks and United Nations Sustainability Goals. Many investors today still do not fully understand the lens or investment thesis of the funds they are investing in, which is why the SEC has raised concerns with the use of the word sustainability in investment vehicles[5] as the term *sustainability* is being increasingly used by a larger number of funds.

---

[5] www.wsj.com/articles/as-funds-jump-on-the-sustainable-bandwagon-regula-tors-raise-concerns-11586103274

www.bloomberg.com/news/articles/2020-03-02/esg-funds-might-soon-have-to-prove-to-sec-they-re-actually-esg

www.sec.gov/files/making-mandatory-sustainability-disclosure-a-reality-white-paper.pdf

www.sec.gov/comments/s7-04-20/s70420-7153853-216459.pdf

www.sec.gov/news/public-statement/lee-regulation-s-k-2020-08-26

# How Emerging Technology (e.g., Blockchain, IoT, AI, Machine Learning) can Provide Journeys of Data to Ensure Trustworthy Metrics and Security

## Measuring and Improving Outcomes With Technology

The sustainability landscape is growing rapidly as more stakeholders engage in ESG interests. Regardless of the role that organizations play in the value chain, every step along the way is driven by data of various different forms. There are many gaps in the data that is collected, generated, and available. In this context, connected cognitive devices that make up the Industry 4.0 landscape are expected to improve the level and quality of data that is captured. This is important in order to better understand the outcomes of initiatives that are put in place to meet the UN Sustainability Goals, or any other sustainability objectives that organizations may have in place.

The various frameworks and methodologies offer context to measure the sustainability components of a given operation against benchmarks or goals. Driving change requires the ability to measure, analyze, and identify problem areas to improve outcomes. Capturing the data at the source in order to better understand the metrics and the impact of this change is implemented through technology.

There are a variety of industries that have begun to use technologies that include the Internet of Things, Machine Learning, big data, robotics, edge computing, and sensors enabled to measure critical information throughout an ecosystem. Two industries that clearly benefit from the use of data monitoring to better measure and influence outcomes are real estate and transportation.

According to the Global Alliance for Buildings and Construction Global Status Report for Building and Construction, it is estimated by the *IEA World Energy Statistics and Balances* and *Energy Technology Perspectives 2020* that buildings currently account for 35 percent of the global energy usage and 38 percent of the global $CO_2$ emissions.[1] Transportation accounts for 28 percent of global energy usage and 23 percent of the global $CO_2$ emissions. Achieving the climate goals that are part of the Paris Agreement Nationally Determined Contributions requires understanding all the components in the value chain in order to implement change and monitor it over time. This understanding requires tools to capture the data and analyze it in order to achieve the objective of a net-zero carbon building stock by the year 2050.

The Environmental Protection Agency[2] reported in 2018 that the largest producers in the United States of $CO_2$ greenhouse emissions are transportation (29%), Electrical production (28%), industry (22), commercial and residential (12%), and agriculture (9%).

In New York City alone, over 70 percent of the greenhouse gas emissions have been from buildings.[3] The city implemented NYC's Local Law 84 (LL84) in 2009, the first energy and water reporting ordinance passed in the United States. Cities are utilizing NYC's LL84 as a model to reduce greenhouse gas emissions in buildings. LL84 requires private buildings over 50,000 sq ft. and public sector buildings over 10,000 sq ft. to report energy and water consumption on a yearly basis. The NYC Energy and

---

[1] https://globalabc.org/news/launched-2020-global-status-report-buildings-and-construction

[2] www.epa.gov/ghgemissions/sources-greenhouse-gas-emissions

[3] www1.nyc.gov/site/sustainability/codes/energy-benchmarking.page

Water Performance Map provides the data for users to understand relative usage and motivate change. Data and analytical tools are enabling visibility and the goal is to use the data to create change.

### Smart Cities and Homes

Smart apartments and smart cities capture information from a variety of different sources to regulate usage and ensure the optimal energy consumption. This is achieved by utilizing sensors, cognitive computing, and networked smart devices at the edge to monitor, capture data, and control energy consumption. Lighting, space heating or cooling, ventilation, hot water, elevators, equipment, and appliances can all be used more efficiently through the use of networked cognitive devices. In addition, smart cities are going beyond the data associated with the infrastructure of connected devices, implementing strategies to improve health care outcomes and other social aspects of their respective ecosystems.

### Transportation

The second largest contributor to greenhouse gas emissions is transportation, yet it is critical for societies to have access to transportation in order to function and thrive. Smart transportation solutions utilizing technology and data from sensors, IoT, machine learning, and artificial intelligence are significantly improving efficiencies for delivery, public transportation, and mobility options and are expanding in scope and sophistication. The ability for communities to participate in the sharing economy, with business models such as ride sharing apps, rely on the existence of networked technologies that enable the location of devices, reservation systems, payment systems, and diagnostics. The growth in technology-enabled mobility solutions will enable the reduction of global carbon emissions, while providing efficient solutions for transportation to jobs and education.

Trucking and delivery fleets now have regulatory requirements to capture data, with the goal of reducing accidents by requiring that data be recorded in order to demonstrate regulatory compliance and reduce driver fatigue. Telematics and IoT devices on fleets have become more sophisticated to facilitate compliance with regulations, which in turn were established to reduce accidents and save lives.

### Blockchain for Governance and Safety

Journeys of Data and Transactions

Data journeys captured immutably in a blockchain enable the trust and transparency required for the verification of safe and legitimate products. Smart networked devices are able to measure the information and record it immutably on the blockchain. It is necessary to measure the outcomes to understand what is working correctly. One simple use of blockchain is to record information immutably so that it can be trusted, which is critical to governance. Waste management, recycling metrics, water usage, and energy consumption data can be captured on an immutable blockchain or distributed ledger to ensure the record of unaltered and accurate information.

Guaranteeing the provenance of food or pharmaceuticals and the temperature they are stored at throughout the journey from production site to consumption site can also be managed through a blockchain. Immutably recording the provenance, identification, location, temperature, and other critical information facilitates the safety of supply chains, which capture these journey data. Distributed ledgers can also connect different components of larger and complex supply chains (e.g., across different jurisdictions, forms of transportation, location) in order to present a full view of the entire journey of a product. The ability to understand the origin, location, and shipping history of specific items ensures the legitimacy and safety of pharmaceutical, food, and a range of other products that are delivered and consumed by a community.

*Figure 7.1 Blockchain journeys of data over time*

Blockchain-enabled marketplaces also facilitate ESG-related exchanges where renewable energy can be purchased or sold, and credits can be banked in an account or wallet on the blockchain. These records streamline access to accurate and updated data to improve transparency for these transactions. There are a number of tokenized advanced renewable energy initiatives that have been built on the blockchain to enable the distributed communities to contribute or utilize energy within a greater electrical grid or through a peer-to-peer network. These operations rely heavily on reliable data.

### Supply Chain Sustainability Solutions

There are numerous technology- and data-driven solutions that are evolving to help industries provide sustainable initiatives with greater transparency. The Global Environmental Management Institute[4] (GEMI) SCS Work Group has engaged a wide range of organizations to capture the data to promote industry dialogue and drive action. The Pharmaceutical Supply Chain Initiative (PSCI), Electronic Industry Citizenship Coalition (EICC), Together for Sustainability (TfS) as the chemical industry coalition are just a few examples of the solutions map that has been created by GEMI. These initiatives are driven by data and utilize surveys, audits, scoring, and rating mechanisms together with qualitative and quantitative solutions to address environmental, ethical, and social transparency at the company, facility, and product levels.

### Data and Cyber Security

As the intangible value of organizations continues to expand, it becomes even more important to understand the threats to the value, which could affect the sustainability of corporations. Intangible assets include intellectual property, rights management, brand equity, software, public rights, agreements, data, and company relationships. According to the AON and Ponemon Institute LLC 2019 Intangible Assets Financial Statement

---

[4] http://gemi.org/solutions/publications/gemi-supply-chain-sustainability-solutions-map/

Impact Comparison Report,[5] 83 percent of the S&P company value is intangible, and 40 years ago, it was only 13 percent. The data in organizations creates value, powers business models, and generates revenue, yet the vulnerability of data security is increasing as hackers find new ways to penetrate organizations, supply chains, and critical infrastructure. More than half of small businesses that experience a breach will go out of business within six months.[6] A University of Texas study[7] indicated that 94 percent of companies that experience a catastrophic data loss will not survive, 43 percent will never reopen, and 51 percent will close within two years.

Cyber risk is a growing risk to the sustainability of companies, communities, and governments. The compromise of personal data within organizations can have a huge impact on people, especially in the health care space. Hackers have increasingly targeted health care data to access patient information associated with specific drugs and use the stolen information to obtain access to controlled pharmaceutical substances. This impacts patients, hospitals, and the community as a whole, where there may be little transparency on the variance between the drugs legitimately prescribed versus the drugs that are sold and consumed.

There are many financial and software companies that have little or no environmental risks, but the cyber risks can be detrimental to the sustainability of organizations, communities, governments, infrastructure, and people. The role of human error in cyber security is the biggest vulnerability. The UK Information Commissioner's Office[8] (ICO) claims that 90 percent of UK cyber data breaches in 2019 were due to human error. As workforces went remote during the COVID-19 pandemic, the level of cyber security and e-mail phishing increased. Google[9] claimed its

---

[5]  www.aon.com/getmedia/60fbb49a-c7a5-4027-ba98-0553b29dc89f/Ponemon-Report-V24.aspx
www.aon.com/thought-leadership/ponemoninstitutereport.jsp

[6]  www.sec.gov/news/statement/cybersecurity-challenges-for-small-midsize-businesses.html

[7]  https://blog.eccouncil.org/the-importance-of-a-disaster-recovery-plan-for-business-continuity/

[8]  https://ico.org.uk

[9]  www.bbc.com/news/technology-52319093

machine learning tools were blocking more than 100 million phishing e-mails a day during the height of the pandemic.

In this context, the FIDO Alliance[10] is one promising innovation that has evolved through an open industry association to create an open and scalable standard to enable more secure authentication and access without the requirement for passwords. The use of cryptography may provide greater levels of security and minimize the vulnerability posed by passwords, which are often lost, stolen, or forgotten.

As the value of intangible assets in organizations continues to increase, the development of cyber security solutions will become even more critical to the sustainability of organizations, governments, and societies as a whole. Cyber security and data governance are integral parts of the ESG metrics, and the financial impact for companies can be devastating.

IBM's Cybersecurity Division[11] and the U.S. Department of Homeland Security reported in December 2020 that sophisticated hackers attempted to steal technology and impact the transportation of the COVID-19 vaccines. Hackers targeted corporate executives involved in the vaccine's refrigeration and transit processes in an effort to gain control by stealing access credentials. The impact on communities of a scenario where the vaccines cannot be delivered could be greater than the impact on the companies themselves. The value that is at risk with these attempts to steal critical information about how to produce the vaccine, test, transport, and distribute it goes beyond material financial risk and shareholder value, it represents a larger risk to society as a whole. The vaccine is critical to saving lives and reviving the economies in these communities.

## AgriTech

There is a direct correlation between AgriTech and the second of the UN Sustainable Development Goals, which is Zero Hunger, in addition to several other sustainability benefits. The ability to increase the yield with less environmental resources, such as much less water or land, offers many

---

[10]  https://fidoalliance.org

[11]  www-nytimes-com.cdn.ampproject.org/c/s/www.nytimes.com/2020/12/03/ us/politics/vaccine-cyberattacks.amp.html

benefits to stakeholders beyond consumers. The demand for food has been increasing as populations grow, while the availability of land, water, and other resources is constant or decreasing. In addition to utilizing 5 percent[12] of the water used in traditional outdoor farming,[13] Aeroponics, for example, offers a closed-loop system, where plants are more effectively able to absorb nutrients, water, and oxygen through the roots, and lighting is programmed for precision. A grower can generate 390 times more productivity from Aeroponics with 95 percent less water than field farming and 40 percent less water than hydroponics. Indoor farming solutions also eliminate risks from climate, storms, pests, or natural disasters, making it a more effective way to increase outputs with higher-quality inputs and less pesticides or chemicals.

Enabling sophisticated AgriTech solutions requires networked sensors to take in the information about the environment. Through connectivity and data, the opportunity to more effectively deliver irrigation, lighting, or supplements as needed, has tremendous benefits. It isn't just about saving energy or resources, but it is about producing higher-quality yields close to the location where they are consumed. This enables the produce to be delivered soon after it is harvested without having to incur costs from food transportation, which also produces emissions.

An October 2020 McKinsey report indicates that yields across AgriTech could improve by 7–9 percent, adding $2–3 trillion to the global GDP[14] over the next decade. They analyzed AgriTech in five use cases, including smart-crop monitoring, drone farming, smart-livestock monitoring, smart-building and equipment management, and autonomous-farming machinery. The value generation from smart-crop monitoring and drone farming offered the greatest amount of new potential GDP growth, especially for Asia, which produces the greatest volume of crops.

---

[12] www.forbes.com/sites/briankateman/2020/07/14/is-the-future-of-farming-indoors/?sh=4b55fd612cc0

[13] www.agritechtomorrow.com/article/2018/05/1-article-for-2018-growing-with-hydroponics-aeroponics-and-aquaponics/10733

[14] www.mckinsey.com/industries/agriculture/our-insights/agricultures-connected-future-how-technology-can-yield-new-growth

There are commercial opportunities to businesses focused on Agri-Tech solutions to offer more efficient solutions to meet the growing food needs with far less environmental impacts. The use of technologies, which include connectivity, drones, sensors, and data science, can even help farmers in developing countries increase their productivity with minimal resource requirements. The growing shortfall of food cannot be fulfilled through traditional outdoor farming methods alone, which require more scarce resources, including land and water. Technology will play a large role in the development of solutions to meet the increasing global need to feed people. Indoor farming also eliminates the natural risks associated with traditional outdoor farming, making it a far more sustainable solution to meet the growing needs for food.

# CHAPTER 8

# Components Needed to Build an ESG Company

## Sustainability Native Companies

The average company historically has not had access to traditional venture capital funds for a variety of reasons. Venture capital funding has remained highly concentrated over time. In the tech space, for instance, funds have been allocated disproportionately toward startups in the Bay Area and the New York, Boston, Washington corridor. Personal networks and relationships with investors have been an important driver of access to venture capital funds. Sand Hill Road in western Silicon Valley, where many major venture capital firms are located, has shown to invest disproportionately in companies located in the vicinity, or companies with which the investors felt some degree of familiarity or relatability. Other metrics have shown significant gender and ethnic gaps for accessing venture capital funding, with women-only teams receiving up to 3 percent of venture funds,[1] while black and hispanic teams received 2.4 percent of these funds from 2015 to 2020.[2] With the staggering influx of ESG-focused investment funds, and the variety of sustainability goals, including diversity, the pool of eligible companies should be expected to broaden. In order to optimize matching these investment funds with eligible companies seeking funding, there are a number of practices that companies could adopt in order to secure and implement an effective sustainability strategy.

---

[1] https://about.crunchbase.com/wp-content/uploads/2020/03/Funding-To-Female-Founders_Report.pdf.

[2] http://about.crunchbase.com/wp-content/uploads/2020/10/2020_crunchbase_diversity_report.pdf.

As entrepreneurs, businesspeople, and companies become more aware of ESG and sustainability metrics, there will be an increase in *sustainability native* companies, which take into consideration the impact of their organization on the stakeholders as well as the investors. These companies have ingrained sustainability into the very core of their business strategy and operations, recognizing it as crucial for their ability to survive over time. This goes beyond philanthropic engagement within the organization, which is tied to operational sustainability goals. It also goes beyond a *check the box* approach to fulfill external sustainability requirements or provide metrics. When an organization prioritizes investing in sustainability, it needs to invest in both people and processes, leveraging data to feed the information, knowledge, and wisdom that make up core components of business decision making.

However, launching a *sustainability native* company does not come without challenges. With the wide array of reporting frameworks, different methodologies for ratings, variety of ESG-related data sources, different investor lenses, and the variety of investment vehicles labeled *sustainable*, it will be important to anchor definitions to the underlying data, financial material impacts, and the value creation for the entire ecosystem. Resilience is not a metric for investors, but it is important for the employees, customers, suppliers, landlords, and all the members of the ecosystem in which a business operates. The diverging metrics and lenses make it more difficult to launch a sustainably native company, as opposed to a digitally native company.

| | Philanthropy | | Social Impact | | ESG | Commercial |
|---|---|---|---|---|---|---|
| | Traditional Philanthropy | Venture Philanthropy | Social Investing | Impact Investing | Sustainable and responsible investing | Traditional, fully commercial companies and investors |
| Focus | Access societal challenges through grants and donations | Address societal challenges with venture investment approaches | Investments with a focus on social or environmental outcomes and some financial return | Investments with the intent to make a social or environmental impact in addition to a financial return | Environmental, Social and Governance data to minimize risks and increase financial returns. | Environmental Data and ESG Risk not part of the investment criteria |
| Return Expectations | Only focused on social returns | Social returns and metrics focus | Social returns and below market average financial market returens | Social returns and Financial Returns | Financial Returns | Only Financial Returns Focus |
| | Social Impact   ⟵——————⟶   Social and Primary | | | Financial Intention   ⟵——————⟶   Financial Returns | | |

*Figure 8.1 Range of sustainable investments*

One can look at companies on a spectrum from traditional commercial entities to philanthropy, yet sustainability isn't philanthropy. It is about quantifying the non-financial aspects of the company to gain insights on how it is managed and how resilient it is to outside forces. In addition, sustainability takes into consideration the external engagement that supports the overall health and growth of the entity, especially over the long term.

There are many facets and layers required for the development of a company that is organized for sustainability. It starts at the board level with the culture, mission, and KPIs that are measured and rewarded throughout the organization. Because it is meant to be overarching and not siloed into a specific department separate from other business functions, a sustainability strategy requires cross-functional cooperation and multidimensional knowledge. This involves virtually every department of an organization, contributing toward the impact of the overall organization in order to maximize synergies, *connecting the dots* to align practices that will create efficiencies and reduce waste. Every layer of the organization needs to be aligned with the sustainability goals and achievements need to be measured against the same goals. The chief sustainability officer and the management team need the support from the board and the leadership to implement the goals and measure the progress throughout both the organization and the ecosystem of partners, suppliers, vendors, distribution channels, etc. The vision and metrics need to be communicated internally and externally using a relevant framework, working with all parties in the ecosystem.

A holistic view of the ESG impact of a business's operations also depends on feedback loops and continual iteration. While sustainability needs to be integrated and managed throughout an organization, beginning from the top, and trickling down through every layer and component of the ecosystem, it also requires feedback loops driven from the bottom. Individuals and entities most in touch with the day-to-day interactions with customers, suppliers, and execution of processes are an invaluable source of information to inform decision makers at the top of an organization of the actual effectiveness of the sustainability strategy in practice. This feedback loop can support the implementation of a sustainability strategy that stems from the right intentions, implemented adequately and in the right order.

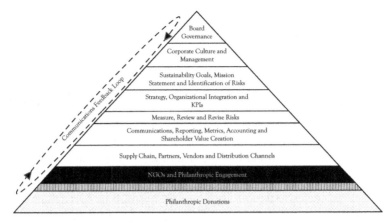

**Figure 8.2  Corporate ESG integration**

© 2022 Cristina Dolan & Diana Barrero Zalles

## Value Generation From Sustainability Opportunities

The UN Sustainable Development Goals identify critical areas where there is a gap, and innovation can help address the needs while creating value not just for the shareholders. Technology, science, connectivity, and data science will offer solutions for many of the goals. AgriTech solutions offer higher productivity with far less resources, including only 5 percent as much water as traditional farming. Online education options are bringing learning to remote areas. While there are other factors that prohibit participation, such as lack of child care, it will be an incremental process to create initiatives that meet these growing needs and adapt to the unique requirements of each region. For example, solutions for clean water, education, food will differ by geography, but the basic innovations may be applicable as a baseline. The ability to work may depend on having access to training, education, and the ability to communicate. Health and well-being are among the most frequently cited UN SDGs. Yet, health care is expensive, requiring highly trained and experienced personnel with access to expensive equipment and treatments, which poses challenges for effective implementation.

There are market opportunities associated with meeting the UN SDGs, and sustainability native companies can create value for all stakeholders, including investors, by building solutions that meet those growing needs. Every startup looks for opportunities where there is growing demand, and many of the UN SDGs identify growing needs that are considered critical around the globe.

## Collaboration and Partnerships

New business models, collaborations, and partnerships will be critical in developing efficiencies that enable greater distributions at price points that are beneficial to all stakeholders. The structures for collaboration and partnering may take many different forms and may focus on specific goals.

For example, Blue Dot Network, a joint venture between the United States, Japan, and Australia for infrastructure investment, promotes a level of transparent, socially, and environmentally sustainable practices through a consortium that certifies infrastructure projects to ensure a higher level of quality. It aims to bring together various stakeholders, including governments, private sector entities, and civil society, through shared sustainability standards for the development of global infrastructure.

### Nongovernmental Organizations (NGOs)

Philanthropic donations are different from internal philanthropic engagement within an organization. While donations may support external organizations that are aligned with the company mission, donations alone do not create a strategy. ESG-minded companies will take a more involved and strategic approach with respect to external organizations supporting common goals by partnering with NGOs or philanthropic organizations, in order to leverage their specific knowledge in ways that promote the achievement of these specific goals.

As companies look to demonstrate a level or social responsibility, partnering with NGOs through public–private partnerships can be an effective way to instill in customers a level of confidence in the company's strategic efforts to behave ethically and engage with all stakeholders beyond just shareholders. There are a number of different national and international NGOs, including the Fairtrade Labeling Organizations (FLO) International (Fairtrade label), Rainforest Alliance, the Marine Stewardship Council, and Forest Stewardship Council, that jointly

brand the validity of sustainability claims for specific products or entities. The number of NGOs that help deal with the complex number of
economic, environmental, and social development issues is also growing.
It is important for these NGOs to maintain their legitimacy within their
scope and brand as they partner with corporations to validate their strategy and actions. The level of research and understanding of community
needs that NGOs have access to provides the opportunity for different
stakeholders to collaborate toward achieving specific goals. NGOS have
access to filling in key knowledge gaps. One of the benefits of working
with NGOs includes their ability to campaign and pave the way toward
effective implementation through their insights from data. Multinational
companies can successfully partner with NGOs to better understand sustainability issues and strategically focus their activities to properly align
with environmental and social policies.

### Lobbyists and Policymakers

The United Nations Principles for Responsible Investing will begin to ask
investors if they have participated in lobbying efforts that are in opposi-
tion with the ESG and sustainability goals of the organization.[3] In addition, investors will have to disclose the internal policies to ensure they are
aligned with their stated positions on sustainable finance in addition to
PRI's six principles. The world's largest sustainable investing group will
begin to report on the alignment of company strategy, internal policies,
and interactions with lobbyists and policymakers starting in 2021.

## The Vision and Strategy

Connecting an organization's strategy with sustainability goals requires
defining the strategy and integrating it at every level or the organization.
While a FinTech company may be committed to climate, most FinTech
companies do not have an environmental impact from their core operations, which largely focus on applying data to provide financial services to

---

[3] www.bloomberg.com/news/articles/2020-12-03/global-sustainability-group-
wants-to-know-who-money-managers-are-lobbying

new communities of users through electronic means. Ancillary operations such as real estate, building maintenance, and daily energy usage indeed may represent a carbon footprint in this matter, but they are not part of a FinTech's business model. Therefore, the governance and labor aspects of ESG would be most integral to the vision and strategy of a FinTech company in general, with awareness of environmental matters in aspects that deal with daily and administrative activities.

For instance, an investment firm needs to have a strategy for investment, but as an organization, it is not manufacturing or creating hazardous waste in the same way that a manufacturing plant would. A FinTech company may have extensive data, which could be used to provide better services or better access to capital through transactional data analysis. Access to capital is critical for economic growth, and therefore, creating a strategy that utilizes the resources of the organization to generate a strategy that benefits the stakeholder, especially the customers and community, is of crucial importance.

## Organizational Structures for Companies Implementing a Sustainability Strategy

Every level of an organization needs to be integrated into the sustainability strategy, to ensure successful and consistent implementation throughout the organization. Board members need to have compensation tied to the achievement of goals, and every level of the organization needs to be trained in these issues, from the C-Suite to the entry-level employees. The chief sustainability officer needs to be put in place with full authority to achieve the established corporate ESG goals, which may involve a series of external relationships as well, including engagement with government and regulatory players. The entire organization needs to be properly aligned. If the chief sustainability officer is only a placeholder in the corporate structure and doesn't have the power to set goals in agreement with the board and senior management, the organization will not position itself well to succeed at achieving sustainability goals. There are many extremely valuable aspects of sustainability that need to be integrated and managed throughout the organization, from data governance and cyber security to employee benefits. The chief sustainability officer has the responsibility of setting these long-term sustainability goals, in collaboration with the board, and enforcing them within the entire ecosystem and throughout their company.

## B Corporations

One example of organizational structure that specifically focuses on for profit companies' commitment to sustainability through a standalone certification is the B Corporation. This class of businesses, across sectors and industries, has committed to the integration of profit and purpose within their strategy. The B Corp certification legally requires them to take into account the impact of their business decisions on the environment, workers, consumers, suppliers, communities. After meeting the transparency, accountability, and performance, and reporting requirements and paying the annual fees to attain the certification, these companies are listed in a public directory that ESG-minded investors may access as they build their portfolios. The B Lab assists companies to attain this certification, and the overall B Corp community is provided with a platform for resource sharing and support. With respect to metrics, the B Impact Score is a relative measure that provides a company's standing among all companies that have provided a B Impact Assessment. It is comprised of Impact Area Scores that also measure a company's relative standing with respect to governance, workers, community, environment, and customers. In many ways, the B Corp designation is considered a gold standard among today's increasingly ESG-focused business practices.

## Data Standardization and Gathering

### Collaboration

There are many different data sources and global reporting frameworks that are used by companies to measure and report sustainability. In September 2020, the most popular frameworks announced a commitment to work together to provide a shared vision for the reporting. These frameworks include CDP, CDSB, GRI, IIRC, and SASB, which in some ways can be complementary because they focus on different ways of looking at the data. On the other hand, the rating companies, indexes, and funds utilize widely different methodologies, which may not be transparent, and they may also purchase different datasets, which provide an added set of different metrics.

### Reporting

Sustainability and ESG metrics are still evolving, and a wide range of different data sources and analytics are being developed. It will take time before broad standardization creates a common vocabulary and set of metrics. Every industry has its own specific characteristics and will need to have these unique profiles represented through the common frameworks.

### Audit

Publicly held organizations may utilize SASB or GRI for reporting, and they also include these disclosures in their SEC filings. SASB reports represent financial materiality of risks, given that for a publicly held organization, risk needs to be disclosed. Some companies may choose to *furnish* financially material ESG and sustainability topics through the Form 8-K (Item 7.01), versus officially disclosing.[4] Another approach would be to work with an auditor to prepare SASB reports and disclose the auditor's opinion in the 10-K. This would limit the company's liability. The auditor who prepared the disclosure and opinion, nevertheless, would not take liability for this matter.[5]

## Improved Corporate Performance

Sustainability and ESG metrics measure the intangible and ethical aspects of companies, which are critical factors for understanding how resilient and prepared an organization is to outside forces. These metrics provide insights on how well a company is run. It goes beyond values and

---

[4] https://corpgov.law.harvard.edu/2019/06/05/sustainability-accounting-standards-and-sec-filings/

[5] https://corpgov.law.harvard.edu/2019/06/05/sustainability-accounting-standards-and-sec-filings/

environmental criteria. For example, the brand of an organization has tremendous value for customer engagement. It takes years and significant sums of money to develop a brand, but one bad decision or strategy can quickly destroy all the value created. Customers can boycott well-established brands if they feel they are not ethical or aligned with their values. Catastrophic data breaches can wipe out small companies within six months, which is why data governance is critical. Engaged workforces are critical to the quality of products and services, such that when skilled labor forces decide to transition away from a company or there is high turnover, it can be very costly for an organization. Companies that don't comply with regulations or the law incur expenses, which can adversely impact operations.

## Investors' Viewpoint

As more investors are attracted to ESG investments with limited clarity on the sustainability lens that is used as the investment criteria, the SEC has raised concerns around the lack of uniform definitions and transparency. There have been record inflows year after year, and yet depending on what industry or role an entity is in, there will be different definitions of what ESG actually means.

### Funds

The word sustainability has many different definitions, which may not be well understood or consistently adhered to by institutional investors or retail investors. The wide array of characteristics that define sustainability needs to be disclosed in a way that the investors can understand within the context of the entire spectrum of definitions. For example, the SHE SPDR SSGA Gender Diversity Index is focused on gender diversity at the senior ranks of large U.S. public companies. Some funds are focused on renewable energy or other areas that may be of interest to investors. There are a large variety of funds that are labeled as sustainable, although the information available to understand these investment strategies may not paint the entire picture on them.

## The Role of the Sustainability Officers in a Fund

With the growing interest in sustainability, it is critical for funds to have a chief sustainability officer to set the strategy, adhere to it consistently, report on it accurately, and prevent any instances of greenwashing. With widely ranging investor definitions for sustainability, it is important for the chief sustainability officer to define the strategy and ensure that it is utilized throughout the organization. Some funds may have a single focus, like diversity in the C-suite, and others may focus on *best of breed* across all industries. The role of a chief sustainability officer within a fund is just as important as a chief sustainability officer at a company, although the lens and process will be different.

# CHAPTER 9

# Company Examples

The industrial revolution has promoted consumer models where the latest and greatest products and gadgets are acquired, while the *old* versions are quickly replaced and discarded. Sustainability is becoming critical to engaging consumers and employing a skilled workforce, which directly impacts the bottom line of an organization. Many organizations are beginning to create sustainable strategies that are focusing increasingly on sustainability, and some have also made announcements about transitioning toward a circular economy. McKinsey predicts that Europe could benefit with a boost of €1.5 billion to €2.5 billion in opportunities by transitioning to a circular economy.[1]

## UN Alliance for Sustainable Fashion

Clothing has become disposable, as fast fashion trends bring price points down as consumption increases, making it an issue for the environment and society.[2] Many garments are worn only a few times and quickly discarded, taking up significant space in landfills where they decompose, or filling excessive donation channels, where they may even be shipped to developing countries and compete with local emerging textile industries. Fashion production makes up 10 percent of human-produced carbon emissions, and 85 percent of all textiles are discarded as waste according to the World Economic Forum.[3] It has the second-largest consumer of the

---

[1] www.mckinsey.com/business-functions/sustainability/how-we-help-clients/circular-economy

[2] www.vox.com/2019/9/12/20860620/fast-fashion-zara-hm-forever-21-boohoo-environment-cost

[3] www.weforum.org/agenda/2020/01/fashion-industry-carbon-unsustainable-environment-pollution/

world's water supply, and washing clothes releases 500,000 tons of micro-fibers into the ocean each year, which is the equivalent of 50 billion plastic bottles. One California study found 13.3 quadrillion plastic microfibers from synthetic clothing in the environment, which are shed during wash-ing. These microfibers easily enter into the oceans and adversely affect marine ecosystems by entering the food chain and habitat.[4] Cotton farm-ing uses a significant amount of water, for example, and it takes 2,000 gal-lons of water to produce a pair of jeans. The dying process used in textiles adds to the water pollution problem by contaminating the equivalent of two million Olympic-sized swimming pools every year. This is one reason why the fashion industry is responsible for 20 percent of all industrial water pollution worldwide. In March of 2020, the UN launched the *Alliance for Sustainable Fashion*[5] to work across the industry to reverse these negative trends. The UN Alliance for Sustainable Fashion is attempting to make the fashion industry sustainable.

## DAVR-BANK—Uzbekistan

The International Finance Corporation, the private investment arm of the World Bank Group, has funded a $5 million program to help Uzbeki-stan's DARV-BANK expand its funding solutions for micro, small, and medium enterprises (MSMEs), particularly women-owned businesses.[6] From a social sustainability standpoint, these groups were already disad-vantaged and disproportionately vulnerable to the financing constraints resulting from the COVID-19 pandemic. The added funds are meant to provide working capital to sustain their operations throughout this challenging period. The World Bank estimates that women-owned busi-nesses make up 23 percent of all companies in Uzbekistan and face a $2.7 billion financing gap, which represents an important barrier for growth. The funding program will foster sustainable and inclusive recovery, safeguarding the jobs and livelihoods of workers.

---

[4] www.theguardian.com/us-news/2020/oct/16/plastic-waste-microfibers-california-study

[5] www.un.org/partnerships/news/launch-un-alliance-sustainable-fashion

[6] https://pressroom.ifc.org/all/pages/PressDetail.aspx?ID=26101

# Indorama Ventures—Thailand

The World Bank's International Finance Corporation took part in the first ever blue loan to Indorama Ventures, a plastic resin manufacturer, to recycle a yearly amount of 50 billion polyethylene terephthalate (PET) bottles by 2025.[7] This $300 million financing package, which is a co-financing divided evenly between the IFC and Asian Development Bank (ADB), will fund an operation that will involve recovering plastic waste from the ocean and landfills from four Asian countries and one Latin American country. Thailand, Indonesia, the Philippines, India, and Brazil are all countries that have struggled with mismanaged plastic waste with serious environmental consequences. The funds of this blue loan, the first to focus on addressing pollution from marine plastic, are certified and tracked. The goal of Indorama Ventures is to recycle 750,000 metric tons of PET globally by 2025, in a process that will create value out of waste and contribute to the circular economy. At the same time, the company will invest in projects to further the use of renewable energy and resource efficiency. These parallel projects include solar panels at facilities in Thailand and India. A waste heat recovery project at the Indonesia PET and fiber manufacturing plant and energy efficiency measures to reduce the carbon footprint of the facility by up to an estimated 25 percent, and other energy-efficiency projects in the manufacturing facilities in Brazil. The overall initiative is also harnessing public–private partnerships at a local level to address marine plastic pollution at a systemic level.

# Mars

When Mars decided to create a plan for sustainability, it realized it needed to improve its supply chain to ensure company wide resiliency. The company needed access to the right crops and the best workers, which implied sourcing from one million smallholder farmers at the tail end of the supply chain.[8] Mars created the Sustainable in a Generation Plan, investing

---

[7] https://pressroom.ifc.org/all/pages/PressDetail.aspx?ID=26079

[8] www.devex.com/news/inside-mars-inc-s-1-billion-pivot-toward-sustainability-91138

$1 billion to deal with numerous issues from climate change, resource scarcity, and poverty within its supply chains. The company had experienced human rights concerns with its cocoa supply chains and realized it needed to make changes. As a result, it decided to tie the need for change into the goals of its core business objectives. Mars prioritized human rights, particularly issues of ending child labor and overall unfair labor practices, throughout their supply chains. Collaboration with NGOs and human rights experts was crucial for implementing the necessary changes. These actions, in the context of issues with child labor laws, have impacted Mars's ability to forge key partnerships with organizations. Eventually the company launched the Farmer Income Lab to better serve the smallholder farmers with which it worked. In conjunction with these social changes, Mars also established goals focused on climate, which included eliminating greenhouse emissions by 100 percent throughout its operations in 80 countries. The company has announced partnerships with the International Fund for Agriculture Development, Oxfam, and Verité to help them implement these goals.

# IKEA

*People and Planet Positive*[9] is the name of the IKEA Sustainable Design Strategy, which is an initiative created to inspire customers to live in more sustainable homes. As a company that has focused on delivering innovative home and furniture products at low price points, it now requires sustainable design and innovation, as well as environmentally friendly transportation and stores. The IKEA *Democratic Design Strategy* is about delivering a high-quality product that is inexpensive, functional, and sustainable. The philosophy is integrated throughout the company to achieve sustainability goals and at inexpensive product price points. To ensure the supply chain adheres to the corporate sustainability values and promotes necessary engagement, IKEA developed the IWAY code of conduct. IWAY was introduced in the year 2000 to define what suppliers could expect from IKEA and clarify the requirements for suppliers of

---

[9] www.ikea.com/ms/en_JP/pdf/people_planet_positive/People_planet_positive.pdf

products and services. This standard involves a number of different categories, from environmental requirements to workers' wages, safety, and health, which includes child labor. The use of sustainable materials that could be recycled or renewed was also part of the strategy. While there may have been criticism about the assembly process for IKEA products, it is critical to minimizing transportation and labor costs. In addition to investments that will enable IKEA to become climate positive, the organization announced it will produce as much renewable energy as it would consume by the end of 2020. It also launched a strategic partnership with Ellen MacArthur Foundation, to become fully circular by 2030 with zero waste.[10] IKEA has run a number of circularity campaigns and events and testing buy-back and resell services in numerous markets in their aim to save energy and reduce waste.

## Blackrock

One of the financial pioneers to announce its commitment to sustainability is Blackrock. In January 2020, this multinational investment management corporation announced its commitment to sustainability as a standard across all its activities involving stakeholders, which include clients, shareholders, employees, and communities. Sustainability is embraced as a means to improve outcomes and manage risk. Larry Fink, Blackrock's CEO, penned a letter on January 14, 2020, championing transparency and encouraging disclosures utilizing the industry-specific Sustainability Accounting Standards Board (SASB) metrics and climate-related risk metrics from the Task Force on Climate-Related Financial Disclosures (TCFD). Setting a new standard for sustainable investing, Blackrock now includes ESG risk analysis in addition to its traditional investment due diligence. This arises from a commitment to limiting investments in companies that generate more than 25 percent of revenue from thermal coal production. In the special Blackrock Investment Stewardship (BIS)

---

[10] www.ikea.com/us/en/this-is-ikea/sustainable-everyday/a-circular-ikea-making-the-things-we-love-last-longer-pub9750dd90

report,[11] the company outlined its approach as the path to creating value for clients with better long-term, risk-adjusted returns. The investment stewardship approach to sustainability goes beyond climate-related issues and includes the full breadth of industry-specific material financial risks associated with all environments, social issues, and governance aspects. Holding directors accountable for sustainability through voting provides an additional level of control over governance and improvement toward implementing and meeting ESG goals. Utilizing advocacy through BIS benefits both clients and investors by increasing awareness and promoting best practices in reporting.

## Microsoft

As a company, Microsoft[12] has received numerous awards for subcategories of sustainability, ESG, and corporate social responsibility that involve social factors, including employee benefits and human rights. The company's sustainability report defines its focus on four key commitments around supporting inclusive economic opportunity, protecting fundamental rights, securing a sustainable future and trust. The commitment to sustainability, ESG, and the UN SDGs is communicated from the CEO of Microsoft and integrated throughout both the organization and the broader ecosystem in which the company operates. These official corporate communications provide a level of transparency that provide clarity for stakeholders to better understand the underlying ESG commitment.

Microsoft has actively taken part in the shared commitment toward achieving the UN SDGs,[13] collaborating with governments and other organizations. While Microsoft's focus will directly impact quality edu-

---

[11] www.blackrock.com/corporate/literature/publication/our-commitment-to-sustainability-full-report.pdf

[12] www.microsoft.com/en-us/corporate-responsibility/recognition

[13] https://onestreamprod.blob.core.windows.net/events/unga/Microsoft%20 and%20the%20UN%20Sustainable%20Development%20Goals%20-%20 September%202020.pdf?sp=r&st=2020-09-24T07:07:56Z&se=2021-10- 01T15:07:56Z&spr=https&sv=2019-12-12&sr=b&sig=WTyTspGpTN7qHXL rZ8Q6hXKraT0eIP92w78H91r0%2FhI%3D

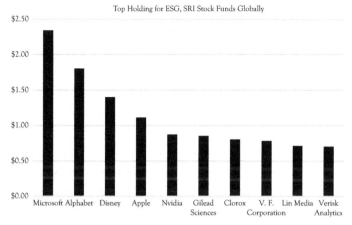

**Figure 9.1  Major ESG holdings**

© 2022 Cristina Dolan & Diana Barrero Zalles

cation (SDG4), decent work and economic growth (SDG 8), climate action (SDG 13) and peace, justice, and strong institutions (SDG 16). The Microsoft Airbank Initiative,[14] for instance, is addressing the UN sustainability goals by providing broadband infrastructure to underserved areas in order to facilitate access to online education and employment opportunities. The company's Digital Crimes Unit has been working with law enforcement institutions since 2010, to find solutions to malware disruptions. According to the company website, this unit has rescued approximately 500 million devices from cybercriminals. Cyber risk is one of the most serious risks that a company can face.

Through partnerships, the company is able to enhance its direct impact into specific communities. For example, by working with ministries of education, academies, and local programs, Microsoft has been able to deliver education to a diverse group of people while enabling an impact across multiple sustainability goals. Certificate and training programs provide a path toward employment and economic productivity. Ultimately, by empowering people, strengthening communities, and protecting the planet, Microsoft will contribute to all these global goals, which are interrelated.

---

[14]  www.microsoft.com/en-us/corporate-responsibility/report

Microsoft is one of the top beneficiaries of sustainability and ESG investment from funds.[15] At the end of 2019, it had $2.34 billion in investment according to EPFR data. The top five organizations with the highest ownership by funds after Microsoft were Alphabet with $1.8 billion, Disney with $1.4 billion, Apple with $1.11 billion, and Nvidia with $0.87 billion.[16] The EPFR data for equity funds includes both active and passive index funds.

For instance, technology companies in general, due to their nature of operations, are not prone to cause major issues with respect to carbon emissions or water usage. This naturally makes them more attractive for sustainability investments, especially from funds that want to avoid climate risk. Yet, some of the largest technology firms have raised concerns with their governance practices, vulnerability to data breaches, and privacy breaches, which involved, for instance, accusations of election interference. These issues, while not climate centered, also present risks that represent financial materiality.

From an investor perspective, it is key to identify the manageable versus unmanageable sustainability risks, not just the relative ESG risks. Many tech companies are focused on contributing to the UN SDGs by utilizing technology solutions to support specific initiatives aimed at closing the gaps. Organizations with agile operations that are able to adapt to unexpected events like COVID-19, data breaches, fires, or electrical outages are considered to be more sustainable when it comes to implementing continuity plans. Implementing business practices that enable this level of sustainability requires a fully integrated strategy from the top down, with priorities that extend beyond short-term financial gains. During the COVID-19 pandemic, the most sustainable technology companies in this respect were able to react quickly by adapting adapt to remote workforces and putting new processes in place to support clients and the overall business.

---

[15]  https://financialintelligence.informa.com/resources/product-content/when-it-comes-to-stock-values-esg-funds-count-for-more#:~:text=The%20force%20is%20with%20SRI,governance%20(ESG)%20criteria%20goals

[16]  https://qz.com/1803716/microsoft-is-the-biggest-recipient-of-esg-rsi-stock-fund-investment/

# CHAPTER 10

# The Road Ahead for ESG

## Convergence and Granularity Across Different Lenses and Definitions

The evolution of sustainability is being accelerated through the creation of new standards and frameworks that are evolving to represent the various facets that represent the investor lenses, company reporting, rating agencies, funds, NGOs, and more. The spectrum of investment methodologies is very broad, offering investors a wide variety of different approaches to supporting sustainability. Some approaches are very narrow in focus, while others offer different interpretations based on various standards and definitions that have been developed.

In the past, disclosures by companies have varied in terms of completeness and focus, which is where the value in the creation of aligned standards will provide greater clarity. This convergence in scope will require alignment and transparency throughout the entire value chain. Convergence alone, however, will not eliminate the need for different reports, as the different lenses toward ESG have a purpose to provide targeted information to various stakeholders with specific interests and requirements. Without setting a common underlying objective for all reporting to provide a detailed level of granularity, it will be impossible to inform investors across the board consistently, regardless of their investment strategy or criteria.

As the various reporting standards come together, as announced by the various standards bodies in 2020, investors, policy makers, board members, employees, and other stakeholders will be provided with a clearer choice of lenses by which to evaluate the decisions they are making.

Spectrum of Socially Responsible, Sustainability, and Impact Investing

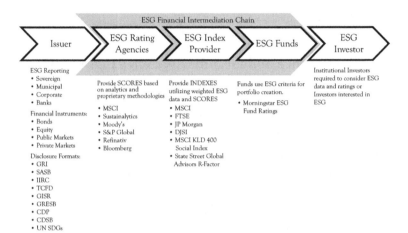

| Traditional Investing | Negative Screening | Integrated ESG | Values Based | Best In Class | Socially Responsible Investing | Value Investment | Impact Investment | Single Focus | Shareholder and Investor Activists | Philanthropy |

United Nations Sustainable Development Goals

**Figure 10.1  Investment strategies for sustainability**

© 2022 Cristina Dolan & Diana Barrero Zalles

ESG Financial Intermediation Chain

Issuer → ESG Rating Agencies → ESG Index Provider → ESG Funds → ESG Investor

ESG Reporting
• Sovereign
• Municipal
• Corporate
• Banks

Financial Instruments:
• Bonds
• Equity
• Public Markets
• Private Markets

Disclosure Formats:
• GRI
• SASB
• IIRC
• TCFD
• GISR
• GRESB
• CDP
• CDSB
• UN SDGs

Provide SCORES based on analytics and proprietary methodologies
• MSCI
• Sustainalytics
• Moody's
• S&P Global
• Refinativ
• Bloomberg

Provide INDEXES utilizing weighted ESG data and SCORES
• MSCI
• FTSE
• JP Morgan
• DJSI
• MSCI KLD 400 Social Index
• State Street Global Advisors R-Factor

Funds use ESG criteria for portfolio creation.
• Morningstar ESG Fund Ratings

Institutional Investors required to consider ESG data and ratings or Investors interested in ESG

**Figure 10.2  ESG financial ecosystem and financial intermediation chain**

© 2022 Cristina Dolan & Diana Barrero Zalles

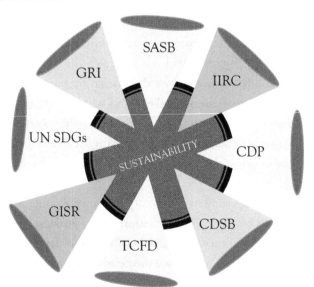

**Figure 10.3  Reporting formats converge into a single standard lens**

© 2022 Cristina Dolan & Diana Barrero Zalles

Underlying convergence, it may even be more critical to ensure the adequate level of granularity that each reporting standard must provide, in order to ensure the necessary level of transparency regardless of the lens adopted to analyze, utilize, or interpret the information. A more standardized level of granularity is crucial to determine ESG risks consistently, regardless of which stakeholders are reading the information and which specific approach is adopted.

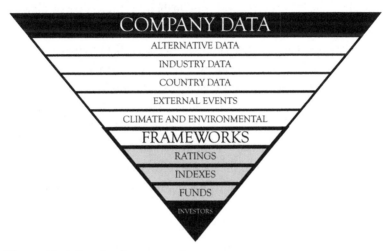

**Figure 10.4 Levels of company data**

© 2022 Cristina Dolan & Diana Barrero Zalles

## A Need for Better Transparency

Transparency into ESG-related risks can be assessed through a variety of different approaches, which can draw on company reports, rating agencies, or funds that are focused on some facet or definition of sustainability. Yet, as these reporting frameworks are different in themselves, they address different components of sustainability and also focus on different aspects of risks to various stakeholders. This leads to a degree of fragmentation that poses challenges for reaching the same consensus when utilizing any of these specific approaches. The methodologies are distinct from each other, with different data sources different approaches. The ratings themselves may not be fully transparent either.

Because the data and methodologies may differ significantly, it can be difficult for investors to fully understand the meaning and impact of

ESG. This makes transparency at the company level even more important for investors. Yet, companies provide reports that take on a variety of formats. The data may not be complete or easily understood, and possibly even biased.

## Technology for ESG Data Management

One of the major concerns with sustainability is the variety of different standards and definitions, making it challenging for retail investors to understand the composition and risks inherent to the funds or securities they are purchasing. The question is how will these many definitions and lenses come together to provide a more cohesive view of sustainability, with the granularity necessary to allow breadth to cover the wide spanning universe of ESG approaches and the depth to provide clarity to every specific area of focus. Every industry may find a different approach to be most adequate, given its specific risks. Therefore, the convergence of standards in the future must be able to adapt to these differences across industries.

Without consistent metrics, it is impossible for organizations to adequately understand the importance of ESG practices and tangible measures required to integrate sustainability within their existing operations, across every process and aspect of the business, and ultimately the entire culture. Otherwise, it is impossible to adequately manage what is not well understood. ESG data, when consistently presented, would enable stakeholders to understand the non-financial performance and the underlying risks.

Here, it is the role of emerging technologies to organize the vast amounts of ESG data and present it with the flexibility and comprehensiveness needed to fit the various needs of ESG initiatives. IoT, for instance, is being increasingly used to record data points across the board, from temperature scores to employee wellness. Blockchain and distributed ledgers can record the data consistently, immutably, and transparently, connecting different sources of data to better provide a holistic view of the various ESG facets of any specific endeavor, across governance, social issues, and environmental issues. Journeys of data can connect the various elements of ESG measures taken by an organization, presenting the entirety of its ESG impact. Artificial intelligence and machine learning can summarize the data and gather valuable insights. Ultimately, better transparency leads to greater accountability, more reliable reporting, and less greenwashing or overstatements. There needs to be an increase in the adoption of data strategies, with an underlying standardization in the scope and timeframe of the data utilized.

## Organizational ESG Strategies

Regardless of the investor approach, the underlying goal is the same, to provide capital to companies that are fundamentally ethical and well run. The risks associated with ESG have material financial impact on companies, and represent a financial risk to investors. The COVID-19 pandemic, for instance, demonstrated the need for non-financial information, which had material financial implications across organizations.

Ethical practices provide for sustainability in terms of ESG requirements and ultimately adequate performance and risk reduction over the long term. This requires proper governance at the board level and throughout the organization, including the adequate handling of data and cyber security. In addition, there need to be standards established for boards to understand how to drive the development of cultures within organizations enforced and enabled from the top.

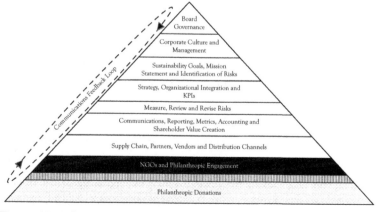

*Figure 10.5  Corporate ESG integration*

© 2022 Cristina Dolan & Diana Barrero Zalles

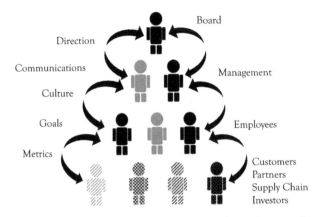

*Figure 10.6 The sustainability culture comes from the top of organizations*

Organizations need to take a top-down approach in order to integrate ESG at all levels, empowering management and employees to implement sustainability strategies. Setting KPIs and metrics to establish achievable goals and measure how the organization implements them is crucial in order to provide transparency and improve results. The culture of an organization comes from the top. The direction and objective need to be defined, supported, measured, and integrated throughout the organization.

### Corporate Management

As corporate boards begin to embrace sustainability, it is important to establish the management responsibilities to execute a sustainability plan. The role of the chief sustainability officer (CSO) needs to be established and empowered, with the ability to implement sustainability initiatives throughout an organization. The CSO's role would be setting goals and metrics across every division, throughout the supply chain, and engaging with NGOs and key partnerships to benefit from targeted expertise. The position of a CSO is more than symbolic, signaling to the organization that sustainability is strategic, provided that the executive is truly empowered to do their job. Metrics are critical to the success of every ESG strategy, ensuring understanding of the necessary changes and their effectiveness. While the responsibilities of a CSO will vary by industry, organizational structure, and dynamics, the evolution of standards at every layer and though every lens will define this role in the future.

## Regulatory Trajectory for Sustainable Finance[1]

Moreover, at the policy and regulatory level, while the SEC is scrutinizing ESG and sustainability funds, there is no enforcement in place or common definitions that would apply across the board. Today, the definition of sustainability is not standardized. As more funds are directed toward sustainable finance, it will be increasingly important to clarify these definitions throughout every level and every lens utilized for ESG initiatives. Transparency and labeling will need to be aligned, and expectations on the level of detail shared needs to be standardized.

This is an issue that policymakers and regulators around the world have become increasingly aware of. There is a growing consensus that all members of the ecosystem from companies to investors need to have a standard that is aligned in order to ensure the clearest understanding and transparency. Policy initiatives and regulation are crucial to ensure alignment, and there is already a trend underway to set requirements for ESG reporting.

### Europe

Europe is leading in sustainable investing and regulatory reforms, including the Sustainable Finance Action Plan and the EU Green Deal. After the COVID-19 pandemic, the EU has pushed for sustainability as the path toward economic recovery. The EU Sustainable Finance Taxonomy[2] was created to help investors understand the environmental sustainability of economic activity. It is the first government wide approach to establish a taxonomy in financial regulation.[3] Funds that are offered to European

---

[1] www.clearygottlieb.com/-/media/files/alert-memos-2020/sustainable-finance-a-global-overview-of-esg-regulatory-developments.pdf

[2] www.unpri.org/policy/eu-sustainable-finance-taxonomy

[3] www.unpri.org/pri-blogs/the-eu-taxonomy-a-generational-shift-for-responsible-investment/4482.article

investors will need to disclose their sustainability methodology, investment thesis, and the percentage of sustainability-focused investments in each respective fund.

## UK

The UK has created its own Green Finance Strategy, which has strengthened the jurisdiction's status as a global hub for sustainable finance, and now requires new climate related disclosures.

### Australia and New Zealand

Australia and New Zealand have can boast allocating the largest percentage of their assets under management focused on sustainable and responsible investing, at over two-thirds.[4] New Zealand is expected to be the first country in the world to establish compulsory climate risk reporting for financial institutions, based on the international framework from the Task Force on Climate-Related Financial Disclosures (TCFD).[5]

### United States

After Europe, the second largest market for sustainable finance is the United States. The SEC has not yet established sustainable investment guidelines, except for the guidelines that require material financial risk disclosures. Progress is underway, however, with a subcommittee of the CFTC having published a report on managing climate risks, recognizing that ESG poses a major risk to the stability of the financial system, that much of its implications are not yet fully understood, that there is insufficient data or analytical tools to manage these risks adequately, and that climate risk in particular can pose a systemic risk and sub-systemic

---

[4] www.thefifthestate.com.au/business/finance/australia-and-new-zealand-lead-in-sustainability-investing-at-almost-two-thirds-of-all-investment/

[5] www.finextra.com/newsarticle/36561/new-zealand-to-make-climate-risk-reporting-compulsory-for-financial-institutions

shocks.[6] It proposes that derivatives markets could better incorporate sustainability risk management measures in order to prevent major shocks, but this requires adequate data.

## Asia

Exchanges in Hong Kong require disclosures for listed companies, and it is expected that companies listed on the Chinese exchanges will align with the government's *Green Finance* strategy. Sustainable assets under management in Japan have increased, making it the third largest geography behind the EU and the United States for sustainable investing. Nikkei 225 index companies have provided ESG disclosures for decades.

## Latin America

Several country-specific initiatives have been launched across Latin America, with various degrees of focus. Ecuador established a Ministry of Environment to design policies and coordinate strategies and programs to safeguard natural ecosystems and ensure responsible uses of natural resources. In Brazil, the Finance Innovation Lab was launched as a national forum for sustainable finance with the goal of developing sustainable financial instruments and introducing regulatory change. Colombia expanded the *Green Protocol Initiative* to include responsible investment, in addition to a focus on green finance and climate risk. In Mexico, the Green Finance Advisory Council was created by the national stock exchange to enable green bonds and more ESG disclosures.

## The Future of Sustainability Native Startups

In the same way that startups have been born as digital native companies, the evolution of sustainability native startups will begin to evolve

---

[6] www.cftc.gov/sites/default/files/2020-09/9-9-20%20Report%20of%20
the%20Subcommittee%20on%20Climate-Related%20Market%20Risk%20
-%20Managing%20Climate%20Risk%20in%20the%20U.S.%20Finan-
cial%20System%20for%20posting.pdf

as standards are better understood. This evolution of sustainability standards will be critical as young organizations engage with larger organizations that are committed to sustainability. Young companies have limited
resources and struggle to adhere to compliance requirements. Without a
clear definition of ESG standards and sustainability requirements, it will
be difficult for small and medium companies to be compliant. Today,
companies that are part of a supply chain, as well as companies that engage
electronically with data within other company networks, need to demonstrate their cyber hygiene through penetration tests. This is one form of
sustainability risk. In the future, there will need to be a more extensive
process to assess the full spectrum of ESG risks within an organization.

# About the Authors

**Cristina Dolan** is an engineer, computer scientist, and entrepreneur who has led the transformation of businesses and built revolutionary products utilizing advanced technologies, including data exchanges, blockchain, cybersecurity, artificial intelligence (AI), Internet of Things (IoT,) telematics, and cloud architectures. In addition to being a cofounder of several companies, including a European value-based health care company, she is an advisor to several cyber security, data, and next-generation cloud computing companies. Cristina was a co-founder of OneMain.com, which grew to be the 10th largest ISP after a successful IPO (Acquired by Earthlink). Formerly, she held executive roles at Disney, Hearst, IBM, Oracle, and Tradingscreen. Recognized as an industry thought leader, she is often engaged as a speaker and has received numerous honors, including 100 Women in Finance, Women to Watch in Crypto and Blockchain, 100 Most Influential Blockchain Women, and Thought Leader in Crypto and Blockchain. The global student coding competition she launched, *Dream it. Code it. Win it*, which is the subject of her TED Talk, has been honored with numerous awards, including a Trader Magazine Charitable Contribution Award, a MIT Harold E. Lobdell Distinguished Service Award, and several Stevie Awards for Best Organization, Best Female Innovator, and Best Executive of the Year. Cristina earned a master's degree from the MIT Media Lab and also holds a Master of Computer Science Engineering and Bachelor of Electrical Engineering. She was a member of the U.S. Bobsled and Skeleton team and earned first place in U.S. Nationals and Empire State Games. She placed second for women at the Skeleton World Cup Championship. She is fluent in Castilian Spanish in addition to her native language, English.

**Diana Barrero Zalles** is the Director of ESG and Climate Tech at Emergents @ Weild & Co., advancing investment banking at the intersection of innovation and strategic governance. She has conducted a national anti-money laundering/countering the financing of terrorism (AML/CFT) risk assessment on virtual assets for the Parliament of Cyprus and compiled regulatory recommendations for blockchain legislation, drawing on global best practices. Diana also runs a blockchain discussion forum at Yale University and has contributed to industry standards for market integrity in crypto trading platforms, central bank digital currencies, and other emerging trends in the digital asset space. Having published market research on stablecoins and market infrastructure, Diana is also a Forbes contributor to educate the investment community about digital assets. Previously, she managed cross-border transactions for international development banks. She is an alumna of the University of Notre Dame and has an MBA from Yale. She was born in Bolivia and is a native Spanish and English speaker.

# Index

## OTHER TITLES IN THE ECONOMICS AND PUBLIC POLICY COLLECTION

Jeffrey Edwards, North Carolina A&T State University, Editor

- *Developing Sustainable Energy Projects in Emerging Markets* by Francis Ugboma
- *Understanding the Indian Economy from the Post-Reforms of 1991, Volume III* by Shrawan Kumar Singh
- *Understanding Economic Equilibrium* by Mike Shaw, Thomas J. Cunningham, and Rosemary Cunningham
- *Business Liability and Economic Damages, Second Edition* by Scott D. Gilbert
- *Macroeconomics, Third Edition* by David G. Tuerck
- *Negotiation Booster* by Kasia Jagodzinska
- *Mastering the Moneyed Mind, Volume IV* by Christopher Bayer
- *Mastering the Moneyed Mind, Volume III* by Christopher Bayer
- *Mastering the Moneyed Mind, Volume II* by Christopher Bayer
- *Mastering the Moneyed Mind, Volume I* by Christopher Bayer
- *Understanding the Indian Economy from the Post-Reforms of 1991, Volume II* by Shrawan Kumar Singh

## Concise and Applied Business Books

The Collection listed above is one of 30 business subject collections that Business Expert Press has grown to make BEP a premiere publisher of print and digital books. Our concise and applied books are for...

- Professionals and Practitioners
- Faculty who adopt our books for courses
- Librarians who know that BEP's Digital Libraries are a unique way to offer students ebooks to download, not restricted with any digital rights management
- Executive Training Course Leaders
- Business Seminar Organizers

Business Expert Press books are for anyone who needs to dig deeper on business ideas, goals, and solutions to everyday problems. Whether one print book, one ebook, or buying a digital library of 110 ebooks, we remain the affordable and smart way to be business smart. For more information, please visit www.businessexpertpress.com, or contact sales@businessexpertpress.com.

Made in the USA
Middletown, DE
10 June 2022